The New York Times

IN THE HEADLINES

Social Media Influencers

APPS, ALGORITHMS AND CELEBRITIES

I0809110

THE NEW YORK TIMES EDITORIAL STAFF

Published in 2020 by New York Times Educational Publishing
in association with The Rosen Publishing Group, Inc.
29 East 21st Street, New York, NY 10010

First Edition

The New York Times
Caroline Que: Editorial Director, Book Development
Phyllis Collazo: Photo Rights/Permissions Editor
Heidi Giovine: Administrative Manager

Rosen Publishing
Megan Kellerman: Managing Editor
Xina M. Uhl: Editor
Greg Tucker: Creative Director
Brian Garvey: Art Director

Cataloging-in-Publication Data
Names: New York Times Company.
Title: Social media influencers: apps, algorithms and celebrities / edited by the New York Times editorial staff.
Description: New York : The New York Times Educational Publishing, 2020. | Series: In the headlines | Includes glossary and index.
Identifiers: ISBN 9781642823578 (library bound) | ISBN 9781642823561 (pbk.) | ISBN 9781642823585 (ebook)
Subjects: LCSH: Social media—Juvenile literature. | Branding (Marketing)—Juvenile literature. | Internet marketing—Juvenile literature.
Classification: LCC HM742.S635 2020 | DDC 302.23'1023—dc23

Manufactured in the United States of America

On the cover: Rachel Talbott, who makes style and beauty videos for 1.1 million subscribers on YouTube, films a video with the help of her husband, Byron Talbott, a chef with 1.4 million subscribers to his YouTube channel, in Santa Clarita, Calif., July 7, 2018; Philip Cheung/The New York Times.

Contents

CHAPTER 3

The Biggest Apps and Sites

CHAPTER 4

International Influencers

CHAPTER 5

A Dangerous Place

Introduction

OVER THE LAST few decades, the entertainment landscape has changed dramatically. The rise of smartphones, tablets and laptops has facilitated social media as a means of connection and entertainment wherever there's a Wi-Fi connection. As a result, people — especially young people — spend a significant amount of time every day online. In fact, a 2019 report from Global Web Index says that figure is two hours and twenty-two minutes per day. This figure has been on the rise for years and will likely continue to increase. This time is spent on messaging or consuming content like how-to information, product reviews, makeup advice, comedy routines, music videos and more. Social media influencers — individuals who have managed to attract the attention of millions — provide much of this content. The articles collected here show that they create entertainment, provide commentary, endorse brands and sometimes inspire the wrath of governments.

The siren song of celebrity is hard for actors, musicians and others to resist. They have created content, and a means of attracting millions of followers, that has garnered the attention of Hollywood, music labels and advertisers of all stripes, all of whom are interested in capitalizing on the influence of someone with a significant social media presence.

Social media apps such as Twitter, Snapchat, Instagram, WhatsApp, Tumblr and Facebook capture much attention, but YouTube is where pop culture in particular thrives. Memes, commentary, web series, tutorials and comedy are all things content creators can use to distinguish themselves. Names like Logan Paul, Jake Paul, Kendall Jenner, Markiplier and PewDiePie rival the popularity of movie stars for many viewers. Influencers are not limited by age either, with some as young as four years old. Internet culture evolves continuously.

AUDRA MELTON FOR THE NEW YORK TIMES

Samia Ali, 4, waits as her parents LaToya and Adam Ali discuss the next scene of her YouTube video, at her home north of Atlanta in John's Creek, Ga., Feb. 5, 2019.

Social media influencers use their clout to cash in on sponsorships and advertising dollars by promoting products to their subscribers. Offline, Internet celebrities can be found at gatherings like VidCon, where they can meet their fans face to face, and hopefuls can learn video techniques and other insider tips.

Outside the United States, social media influence can be more political in nature. China, in particular, hosts staggeringly popular social media platforms like Weibo, a Twitter-like microblogging site, messaging app WeChat and live-streaming site Douyin (or TikTok). Yet China is also a center of censorship. Internet celebrities must toe the line or run afoul of government restrictions. Influencers in places such as Pakistan have been murdered for challenging traditional cultural norms. In New Zealand, a mass murderer took to Facebook to livestream his crimes — and suggested that people should subscribe to PewDiePie's YouTube channel.

Social media influencers are not immune to the dangers of the digital sphere either, as cyberbullies and malicious hackers have attacked celebrities and regular viewers alike. Another component of having a significant social media presence has to do with the pros and cons of individual platforms: What might seem like innocent changes to a platform's revenue policies can result in reduced income for content creators. In one extreme instance, YouTuber and self-described animal rights activist Nasim Najafi Aghdam retaliated against the platform's policies by attacking YouTube headquarters with a gun, shooting three people before killing herself. More commonly, algorithm changes, feuds between influencers or "being canceled" can affect an influencer's following, advertising partnerships or revenue.

Today, advertising and social media influence go hand in hand, and the constant evolution of relationships between disparate companies and individuals can be difficult to track. The ever-changing digital landscape consistently has influencers creating new and different ways to both entertain and cash in on the lucrative rewards of their celebrity.

CHAPTER 1

The Internet Celebrity Culture

The culture, terminology and offerings that become popular on the Internet have a flavor all their own — and create their own celebrities. Such celebrities can be as young as four years old, though most are in their teens or early twenties. Searching for fame on accessible outlets like YouTube is common for many actors, comedians and others — and with that fame comes influence.

ROFLThing Draws the Internet Celebrities

BY JENNA WORTHAM | JAN. 25, 2009

THERE'S FAMOUS, AND then there's Internet famous. The latter, often obtained accidentally, is often the result of a popular video, catch-phrase, image or idea spread virally through the Web.

To explore the meaning of both and the nuances in between, hundreds of Web celebrities, bloggers, video creators, fanboys and girls crowded into downtown Manhattan at Santos Party House on Saturday for ROFLThing NYC, a conference devoted to dissecting and celebrating the people behind popular ideas on the Internet. ("ROFL" is Internet shorthand for the phrase "Rolling on the Floor Laughing," commonly used during instant messaging or on message boards.)

ROFLThing NYC is an offshoot of ROFLCon, a three-day conference spearheaded by then-Harvard undergraduate Tim Hwang in

April in Cambridge, Mass. Since then, Mr. Hwang, along with his fellow organizers, has been hosting smaller satellite events, called ROFLThings, around the United States.

Attendees received swag bags containing stickers, prophylactics featuring an infamous Internet image and cans of Brawndo, an energy drink featured in the 2006 dark comedy "Idiocracy." At the bar, free lattes were served with images printed in burnt sugar on the foam, including a 1UP mushroom from the Super Mario Brothers video game and the smiling mug of Mr. Hwang.

Saturday's event featured talks by Charlie Todd, founder of Improv Everywhere, a group that organizes impromptu, harmless pranks. One of his better-known choreographed events involved recruiting more than 200 New Yorkers to simultaneously freeze in place in Grand Central Station for five minutes.

There were also two presentations on Web art: "Firefox Art," detailing the more creative types of Web add-ons to Mozilla's platform and a talk by Bre Pettis, founder of hacker art collective NYCResistor, who discussed rapid prototyping technology. Also in attendance were several members of the geek elite, including Jay Maynard, better known by his nickname Tron Guy for a spandex bodysuit rigged with blue lights to resemble the main character from the 1982 Disney movie "Tron"; Rex Sorgatz, a well-known blogger; and Alexis Ohanian, co-founder of social bookmarking news site Reddit.

Although ROFLThing NYC was just a one-day affair, organizers plan to keep hosting the smaller events throughout the year and hold a larger, second edition of ROFLCon in fall 2009.

Internet Memes 101: A Guide to Online Wackiness

BY DAVID POGUE | SEPT. 8, 2011

IN THE OLDEN DAYS, it was simple to keep up with pop culture. There were only three channels on TV, and everybody saw the same shows at the same time.

These days, of course, not so much. There are 500 channels on TV, and you can watch anything at any time. That doesn't mean, however, that we no longer have a common pop-culture base. We do — it's just moved online. Show me somebody under 20, and I'll show you someone who can laugh at "Friday," sing the "Bed Intruder Song" or "plank" in an incongruous place.

But there are plenty of other people who aren't getting the references at cocktail parties and in the late-night comedians' monologues. And a certain percentage of those out-of-the-loopers might wish they had a single, concise cheat sheet of the most important Internet memes (fad concepts).

Today's your lucky day. After consulting Know Your Meme, my Twitter followers (I'm @pogue) and my own three under-20 offspring, I've put together this essential list of Memes You Should Know.

MODERN VIDEOS

Much of online pop culture lives and dies on YouTube. Over and over again, the videos most likely to go viral are the ones that incorporate catchy music, humor and spectacle — preferably all three.

"Friday." In March, a 13-year-old girl named Rebecca Black released a YouTube music video. It became a sensation, with 167 million views — not because it was good, but because it was screamingly bad. With 87 percent thumbs-downs, it's the most disliked video on YouTube. Sample ultra-banal lyrics: "Seven a.m., waking up in the morning ... Gotta have my bowl, gotta have cereal..."

"Friday" wound up being performed by Stephen Colbert and the cast of "Glee," making several pop-music charts and, most deliciously, inspiring dozens of YouTube parodies. Some of those have themselves become megahits. In the warped "Brock's Dub," for example, the original audio is replaced with a Christopher Walken impersonation (warning: obscenities).

"Bed Intruder Song." In July 2010, an Alabama news station, WAFF, reported an attempted rape. The intended victim's brother, the eccentric and animated Antoine Dodson, spoke directly to the camera: "He's climbin' in your windows, he's snatchin' your people up… so y'all need to hide your kids, hide your wife and hide your husband cuz they're rapin' e'rybody out here!"

Mr. Dodson's performance was Auto-Tuned into melody and set to incredibly catchy music by the Gregory Brothers (see below). The result was the most-watched noncommercial YouTube video of 2010, inspiring over 2,500 people to record their own versions of the song, including a marching-band edition.

"Hitler Finds Out" (a k a "Downfall"). For some weird reason, a scene from the 2004 German movie "Der Untergang" has become fodder for a huge array of YouTube parodies. In the scene, Hitler has a breakdown, screaming at his generals; Internet wiseacres love to add subtitles that make it seem as though he's reacting to some trivial, modern-day development.

There's actually a YouTube "HitlerRantsParodies" channel. Here, among hundreds of others, you'll find the spoofs where Hitler learns that Twitter is down, that Sarah Palin has resigned the governorship and that he's been banned from Xbox Live.

The new classics. Your education is not complete unless you've also witnessed the bizarre goofiness of modern-day YouTube classics like "Cows & cows & cows," "Double Dream Hands" and "Honey Badger" (watch both the original and the overdubbed parody). No explanation of these will be provided here, because there is no possible explanation.

CLASSIC VIDEOS

New videos go viral every day, but your online pop-culture education would not be complete without an appreciation for these immortal older videos:

Dramatic prairie dog. The funniest five-second video on YouTube. As three evil chords play, the prairie dog turns to face the camera as it zooms in. That's it.

David After Dentist. A home video in which a 7-year-old boy (David DeVore Jr.), still under the effects of oral-surgery anesthetic, hilariously wigs out at his sense of spacey disorientation.

Numa Numa Dance. In 2004, a chubby young man named Gary Brolsma recorded himself sitting in front of his computer, wearing headphones and dancing/lip-syncing to a Romanian pop song called "Numa Numa". There's such earnestness and charisma in his performance that you can't tear your eyes away; his video, and copies of it, have been viewed 700 million times.

Keyboard Cat. It's just a silly 1984 video of a cat wearing a shirt and playing the piano (its paws manipulated offscreen by its owner). But its cultural impact has included 17 million views, cameos in video games and awards shows, and appearances on T-shirts. Above all, Keyboard Cat has become famous as a "Play him off, keyboard cat!" clip tacked onto the end of over 4,000 other videos (people falling, George W. Bush pelted with shoes, and so on).

PRANKS

The trend of the Web as the source of all humor continues with trends like these:

Rickrolling. It's an online bait-and-switch. You send a Web link to someone, promising something exciting or compelling ("Is this you!?") — but the link actually takes your victim to a YouTube video of Rick Astley's 1987 music video, "Never Gonna Give You Up." That's it. That's the joke. Ha! You've been Rickrolled! (See the Wikipedia article "Rickrolling" for an astonishing list of high-profile rickrolls.)

Planking. Here's one of the few Internet memes that has a real-world component. In it, people take photos of themselves lying, face down, expressionless, arms at their sides, in strange locations: on rooftops, cars, trees and so on — and post them on Facebook.

The practice was originally meant to be a comment on the cliché of the usual tourist photo — facing front, fake smile, landmark in the background — but has now become, well, just a weird fad.

MEMES

Sometimes, Internet memes aren't videos or acts, but just ideas that get passed around. Some classics:

LOLcats.com. A Web site where people superimpose captions on cat photos. Always the same font, always the same weird broken-English catspeak syntax. And darned funny.

Chuck Norris Facts. In this meme (immortalized by Web sites and even books), people pass around hyperbolic references to the virility and strength of Chuck Norris, the movie and TV action actor.

"Chuck Norris won American Idol using only sign language," goes one. "Chuck Norris can cut through a hot knife with butter." "Death once had a near-Chuck Norris experience."

YOUTUBE STARS

YouTube is a talent discovery machine. Dozens of talented performers have become full-time YouTube video makers; the most popular of them produce weekly mini-masterpieces of comic silliness and sarcasm.

They include Ray William Johnson, the #1 most-subscribed-to YouTube personality, with over a million followers; Nigahiga, whose humor is perfectly suited to the middle schoolers who adore him; and Mystery Guitar Man, a virtuoso on both every musical instrument and his video-editing software.

Then there are the Gregory Brothers, the four Brooklyn musicians responsible for "The Bed Intruder Song" and other Auto-Tuned video megahits, including "Double Rainbow" and "Backin' Up."

The Gregory Brothers' YouTube success has brought them an agent, an Academy Awards appearance, an iPhone app and a development deal for a new Comedy Central TV show.

Yes, that's right: among its many other accomplishments, the new-media meme machine is perfectly capable of producing material for the old media. Next thing you know, you'll turn on your TV set, spot some gifted musician or comedian — and be grateful that you were culturally tuned-in enough to recognize them from their humble beginnings online.

Finding Fame, and Sometimes Fortune, in Social Media

BY STEVEN LECKART | SEPT. 26, 2012

SOCIAL MEDIA HAVE made it easier than ever to catapult from obscurity to prominence. In recent years, the Web has blossomed into a more egalitarian version of "American Idol," where nobodies compete for attention alongside somebodies.

Today, a teenager posting webcam videos to YouTube can get a movie deal ("Fred: The Movie"). A 30-something posting one-liners on Twitter can land a TV show on CBS ("$#*! My Dad Says"). Bloggers creating Internet memes are being offered book deals at a dizzying pace.

However, alongside breakout Web celebs — not to mention actual celebrities with huge online followings like Rihanna and Katy Perry — there's a new class of microstars who are highly popular and viral, but have no aspirations of going Hollywood.

How they became Internet-famous — and made comfortable incomes — offers insights to those who are unsure of how to use Twitter, Instagram or Tumblr to promote themselves or their projects.

THE CELLPHONE QUIPSTER Like many teenagers, Joey Mueller, 19, spends much of his time texting on his iPhone. But when he taps out a 140-character message and presses send, he's talking to nearly 400,000 people.

Mr. Mueller created his Twitter account, @itisjoey, in 2010. as he was traveling to compete at the World Horseshoe Tournament in Cedar Rapids, Iowa. He figured using Twitter to comment from a big event might help him draw an audience.

"I didn't get any followers or anything," he recalls, "I guess it wasn't interesting."

Now a sophomore majoring in graphic design at the University of Minnesota, he decided to avoid personal messages and focus on observational humor. A sample @itisjoey post: "Nancy Grace is the human equivalent of caps lock."

Mr. Mueller said his personal Tumblr Web site already had 75,000 followers. He added a link to his Twitter account. Immediately, his follower count jumped. Then a curious thing happened: the numbers kept climbing. In 2012, he hit 440,000.

"I'm not sure why," he said. "Sometimes I think I got lucky."

Mr. Mueller said he had never purchased followers. He said that posting from noon to 6 p.m., when people typically spend more time online, helps. He also routinely adopts popular hashtags, especially political ones, which he said helped get him retweeted by organizations including Move On. The fame hasn't gone to his head, he said, or at least his parents keep him down to earth. "They're like, 'You know, you're not really famous. Stay in school.' "

THE TATTOO CHRONICLES Kimber Turner was bored. In the spring of 2008, when she was a 22-year-old journalism major at Middle Tennessee State University in Murfreesboro, Ms. Turner completed all of her courses online. Which is to say, she spent a lot of time on her laptop.

Ms. Turner started killing time online by collecting found images of tattoos borrowed mostly from body modification Web sites. She decided to post the photos on a Tumblr account she hastily titled with an obscenity common among youthful creators of Tumblrs, personalized Web pages where ephemera is deposited. In a few months, Ms. Turner had 300 followers. Other Tumblr users began e-mailing pictures and explanations of their own tattoos to her.

"Everybody wanted their story out there," Ms. Turner says, "People just really liked how interactive it was."

In 2008, she said, she received 200 submissions a day. Four years later, she gets 350 a day, she said. Images are contributed by fans all over the globe.

Today, Ms. Turner has more than 695,000 followers. For comparison, when Texts from Hillary went viral on Tumblr earlier this year, it attracted 45,000 followers in a week.

Her secret? Volume. She publishes about 50 photos a day, one every 30 minutes, to keep fans coming back. She also follows Tumblr's other popular users.

"There's so many people on Tumblr who post all sorts of random things," Ms. Turner says. "Having a focus really lets people connect, and it's a great way to stand out."

Although she took various odd jobs after graduating in 2011, including one as a receptionist for a seamstress, ads on the site earn her $60,000 annually, she said.

"When I realized it could very well just be a full-time job, I nearly had a heart attack," she says, "Now I make more than my parents."

THE HYPERLOCAL RADIO D.J. Jaime Black, 29, says he has been a "huge radio nerd" since he was 15. He cut his teeth at an alternative rock station, Q101 in Chicago, where he graduated from an internship to a weekend producing job.

On the side, in 2005, he began podcasts about Chicago's underground music scene. Called Dynasty Podcasts, the episodes — 10- to 15-minute interviews Mr. Black records with local artists and club owners — were made available as MP3s on his Web site. The response was modest.

Five years later, when he created a SoundCloud account, he saw just how broad his reach could grow. He has amassed more than 43,000 followers on the audio-sharing Web site, which has been called the "YouTube of audio."

"I was very fortunate to get there early," Mr. Black says of SoundCloud, which claims to have 20 million users. "I might have beat some of the larger radio stations to SoundCloud. I didn't see that much non-music content when I started."

Today, Mr. Black posts two to 11 shows a week, which he records with a hand-held Olympus digital recorder. His philosophy is, "Make it easy for people to discover the content and know right away what it is."

"I'm sharing it on Instagram, Twitter, Tumblr, Pinterest," he says. "I don't just post things without putting some effort into the presentation. All the imaging is uniform. All the metadata is uniform."

In 2011, Mr. Black started running local event promotions, just like a radio station. He turned Dynasty Podcasts into a full-time job and said he earned $500 for one hour of work.

"A few years ago it was like, 'Oh, how cute, you have a pretend radio show,' " Mr. Black said. "And now, we just did a promotion with Supercuts."

THE METROPOLITAN PAPARAZZO Whenever a new digital service is started, there is a race to claim user names. In January 2011, Liz Eswein, then a senior at New York University, claimed one of the better Instagram user names: @newyorkcity.

"People have said, 'Oh, I thought the city of New York was running it.' " Ms. Eswein laughs, "It's like, nope, it's just me."

It is difficult to tell that the feed is not maintained by someone in the mayor's office. Ms. Eswein, 23, posts only photos taken in and around the city. Using her iPhone 4S, she sticks to snapshots of familiar landmarks like the Statue of Liberty and Central Park, and pictures taken at local events like the United States Open and New York Fashion Week. One of Ms. Eswein's recent snapshots of the Plaza Hotel earned 13,330 likes. She said she often saw comments from users across the United States and as distant as Australia, South America and Greece.

"Instagram is a great way to see different parts of the world through your phone," she said, "Everyone has a special place in their heart for New York City."

Soon after starting the account, Ms. Eswein began attending local Instawalks, where users gather to socialize and take photos. The gatherings publicized her account among the app's power users.

By April 2012, @newyorkcity had 195,000 followers. It jumped to 422,000 after the release of an Instagram app for Android phones. (For some perspective, Lady Gaga's account currently has about 440,000 followers.)

In March, Ms. Eswein founded a business with two Instagram users. They now consult with brands, including Evian and Samsung, that are looking to engage users on Instagram.

Does she also keep a personal account on Instagram? "Yeah, but I don't use it at all," she said.

Glued to the Tube

BY AMY O'LEARY | APRIL 12, 2013

HERE ARE SIX other YouTube superstars you may not have heard of:

SMOSH

9 million subscribers

2.2 billion views

The comedy duo Ian Hecox and Anthony Padilla, both 25, are known for their slapstick sketches, including a series called "Harry Potter Deleted Scenes" that depicts young wizards behaving badly.

RAY WILLIAM JOHNSON

8.3 million subscribers

2.3 billion views

Mr. Johnson, 31, makes viral videos that recap, yes, other viral videos. Posted Tuesdays, his videos also feature celebrity drop-ins like Robin Williams and Margaret Cho.

NIGAHIGA

7.8 million subscribers

1.4 billion views

Ryan Higa is a 22-year-old comedian who gained YouTube fame with lip-sync videos. He now rants on topics like, "How to Be Emo" and "How to Be Gangster."

PEWDIEPIE

6.6 million subscribers

1.4 billion views

PewDiePie is the YouTube alias of Felix Kjellberg, a 23-year-old Swedish video gamer who records himself reacting — often in horror, sometimes with tears — to various games.

HOLA SOY GERMAN

5.7 million subscribers

413 million views

Hola Soy German (Hello I Am German) is the YouTube channel of German Garmendia, a 22-year-old comedian in Chile who has imported this video genre to a Spanish-language audience.

MICHELLE PHAN

3.6 million subscribers

694 million views

Michelle Phan, who offers makeup and beauty tutorials, is the second-most-subscribed-to woman on YouTube after Jenna Marbles. Popular videos include "Barbie Transformation Tutorial" and "Lady Gaga Bad Romance Look."

How Jake Paul Set the Internet Ablaze

BY ALEX WILLIAMS | SEPT. 8, 2017

The 20-year-old YouTube megastar is mining a summer of controversy to build a social media empire.

LOS ANGELES — With grave concern, a television reporter for KTLA described the mayhem in the upscale Los Angeles neighborhood of Beverly Grove in July: The residents of a graffiti-marred, $17,000-a-month white contemporary house, led by a 20-year-old "social media megastar" named Jake Paul, had turned this "tightknit community" into a "war zone."

"A recent stunt involved tossing furniture into an empty pool and setting the pile on fire," the reporter informed viewers. "Neighbors said flames eventually grew higher than the house."

With the news crew still mingling outside, Mr. Paul bounded out of the house, his peroxide-blond hair flopping, trailed by a squadron of artfully coifed teen-heartthrob types. They mocked the reporter's fusty brown oxfords, and whooped as their leader clambered onto the roof of the KTLA van ("Jake, I wouldn't do that," the reporter warned), where he stood triumphant — symbolically, at least — over the old-media landscape.

Facing a scene that looked like a boy-band version of "A Clockwork Orange," the reporter grilled Mr. Paul: "They say that you have created a living hell out here, that you've created a circus."

Mr. Paul responded with a smirk: "But people like going to circuses, right?"

The stunt made global headlines and turned the YouTube prankster into a social media villain. A "moronic menace to society," Canada's National Post called him; an "absolute terror," according to Mashable; "the worst person on earth," in the words of Deadspin. But to Mr. Paul and his devotees, who track his pranks religiously and call themselves "Jake Paulers," the incident was something much greater.

"It was gold," he said.

He has 10.5 million subscribers on YouTube, and seemingly five million haters. This high school dropout from Ohio has already outlasted Vine, the short-form video platform that gave him his first taste of fame; survived an ill-fated turn as a Disney star; cut a rap anthem ("It's Everyday Bro") that became, simultaneously, one of the most viral and reviled songs on the internet; and established himself in the eyes of grown-up America as an embodiment of everything that is wonderful and horrible about Generation Z.

And all that, basically, has been a warm-up act. Even as controversies stack up and the #jakepaulisoverparty hashtag circulates, Mr. Paul is leveraging a Johnny Knoxville taste for outrage with mogul-size ambition to build an empire out of that sprawling Beverly Grove house, serving as a Svengali and star maker to the YouTube stars of tomorrow. Think of it as a factory of social-media talent, a scrubbed, web version of Berry Gordy's Motown Records for preteens.

A genius or a jerk? A punk or a prophet? In a media landscape where clicks are money, does it even matter?

"I know it's a cliché," Mr. Paul said in a rare interview at his home two weeks ago. "But, like, literally, I want to create an empire of dozens of talent under me, to take my power and multiply it so that I become bigger than myself."

"My personal goal," he said, "is to be a billionaire."

FROM DISNEY TO YOUTUBE RAPPER

Mr. Paul, who is arguably the most polarizing personality on YouTube, remembers the moment back in Westlake, Ohio, when he told his parents, Greg Paul, a real estate agent, and Pam Stepnick, a nurse, that he planned to skip his senior year of high school and move to Los Angeles with his brother, Logan, to pursue fame.

JAKE MICHAELS FOR THE NEW YORK TIMES

Jake Paul, center, the 20-year-old YouTube star, performing a stunt.

It was not as crazy as it sounds. He and Logan, who is two years older, had already established themselves as breakout stars of Vine, that Ritalin-addled showcase of six-second comedy snippets that, for a moment, seemed like it might swallow teen culture.

"There was real-life opportunity to make a career for ourselves, for the rest of our lives," he said. "We were working with brands and advertisers. I was, like, 17 years old, making more money than my parents."

For the Paul brothers, Hollywood proved to be anything but a boulevard of broken dreams. Leveraging their millions of social media followers, along with their well-honed skills for rubber-faced comedy and ambulance-worthy stunts, each started a YouTube vlog that became explosively popular. Web fame soon led to mainstream work on television: Jake earned a regular role on the Disney Channel sitcom "Bizaardvark," playing — what else — a goofy young social media star.

But while Logan set his sights on becoming "the biggest entertainer in the world," as he put it to Business Insider, his younger brother sought a career beyond the camera's glare. He wanted to become the Dr. Dre of social media.

"I saw what he did," Mr. Paul said of that N.W.A. rapper turned mogul, "how he was a celebrity himself, and then he took that, brought people under his wing, taught them how to make music, and then put those people in front of his audience. Out comes Eminem, 50 Cent, Snoop Dogg, Tupac. And then he used that network to launch different companies and go into merchandising, obviously his big one being Beats by Dre."

Jake Paul was suddenly Jake Paul, Inc., the head of Teen Entertainment and Media Kingdom, or TeamDom, a company he started this past January centered on a talent label called Team 10. The team, which never actually had 10 members (but who's counting?) was made up of an ever-evolving crew of teen idol types under contract to Mr. Paul, who sought to turn them into web stars.

Not yet old enough to legally drink alcohol, Mr. Paul was now a mix of talent manager, executive producer, life coach and motivational guru to a constellation of rising YouTube vlog stars, several of which had more than two million subscribers. He also acted as a resident adviser, given that a half-dozen of them bunked full-time at the social media "incubator" that was the Team 10 house.

Before long, the venture was drawing interest from more than just angry neighbors. Heavyweight investors like Ron Burkle and Gary Vaynerchuk jumped aboard. In Dr. Dre fashion, Mr. Paul debuted a merchandise line, Fanjoy.co, hawking a collection of skater-ish sweatshirts and T-shirts to the swelling army of "Jake Paulers."

Even so, the tent pole property of Team 10 was, and remains, Mr. Paul's daily vlog, a seven-day-a-week, web-based reality show consisting of "Jackass"-style stunts, "Punk'D"-style pranks and "Real World"-style domestic drama involving life around the Team 10 house.

Not that those Generation X references would mean much to Mr. Paul's target audience, who were born in the George W. Bush or

Barack Obama years. And the brand stakes its existence on keeping these attention-challenged adolescents coming back for more.

Because it really is every day, bro — to cite Mr. Paul's mantra. It has been for more than 335 straight days and counting.

That is why Mr. Paul decided one day in May, on a whim, to transform himself into a rapper. "I woke up, and I was like, 'What if I make a song today, and make a music video for it, all in one day?' " he said.

As Mr. Paul tells the story, he spent a few hours tracking down a producer and booking a studio, maybe 30 minutes scribbling out some rhymes for himself and his crew, and another few hours to record the track. That afternoon, Mr. Paul secured a glassy hilltop mansion in Coldwater Canyon as a location to shoot the video (it seemed like the perfect parody location of a cliché hip-hop video, he said) and rustled up a white Lamborghini as a prop.

"To me, the whole thing was a joke," he said. "I was like, I'm going to morph into a rapper and just go for it, 100 percent."

Flexing like a "Friday Night Lights" extra and grabbing his crotch like LL Cool J circa 1987, Mr. Paul threw himself into the role, rapping: "It's everyday, bro, with the Disney Channel flow, 5 mil on YouTube in six months, never done before."

No one was going to confuse it for Kendrick Lamar. But the pre-tweens of the Jake Paul Army scarcely cared.

Released on May 30, "It's Everyday Bro" shot to No. 2 on iTunes. Three months later, the video has been viewed more than 115 million times on YouTube. At a recent live performance, Mr. Paul rapped the first line, then held the microphone toward the audience. The crowd of 12,000 finished the song a cappella. "They knew every word," Mr. Paul said in astonishment, "even the Martinez twins' lines in Spanish."

ONE DAY WITH TEAM 10

By 9 a.m. on a sweltering Tuesday in late August, a cluster of teenage girls was already padding around the leafy sidewalk outside the angular white stucco house near Hollywood's Fairfax district where

Team 10 is based, waiting for a chance to squeal "Jake!" or "Erika!" or "Kade!"

Strolling around the house that morning, it was not hard to find evidence of the youthpocalypse portrayed in media reports. In the backyard, next to a giant trampoline, an overturned office chair teetered at the edge of the "bonfire" pool, now filled with water, but with a flat-screen television lying facedown on the bottom.

A spirit of anarchy, however, was noticeably absent. Inside the cavernous and scarcely furnished main floor, the house felt more like the office of a Silicon Valley start-up than a modern, teenager-filled "Animal House." Handwritten notes exhorted housemates to tend to their trash. A mini-basketball hoop hung on one wall. A pink tie-dyed banner emblazoned with the Team 10 logo blanketed another.

At an hour when some corporate Angelenos were still idling on the 405 freeway, Team 10 was hard at work. Justin Roberts, known as "the Freshman," quietly labored behind a computer monitor. At 15, the home-schooled student still lives with his parents. That does not mean he is denied the Team 10 halo effect. The rap star Drake recently dropped in on his birthday party at the nightclub Tao.

The team matriarch, Erika Costell, a 24-year-old model from Michigan, mingled nearby in workout gear. Half of the Team 10 power couple "Jerika," she has three million YouTube subscribers and got a big boost from her "wedding" video with Mr. Paul, "We Actually Got Married..." in June, which has attracted 21 million views, even though they actually did not get married. ("We're not even actually dating," Mr. Paul explained later that day. "It's like the WWE. People know that's fake, and it's one of the biggest things of entertainment.")

Sitting quietly on the blond-wood staircase was Mr. Paul, stroking his Belgian Malinois puppy, Apollo, who has 1.4 million Instagram followers. In conversation, Mr. Paul seemed 180 degrees from the fist-pumping, high-fiving uber-bro known to millions.

"Off camera, I'm, like, chill and very laid-back," Mr. Paul said, speaking in the polite, deferential tones of a student talking to a guidance counselor. "I don't know if the word is 'shy,' but 'reserved.' I'm always thinking."

The daily vlog is "an extreme version" of reality television, he said, and the Jake Paul who is the current scourge of greater Los Angeles is merely a character. "Literally, by saying the word 'bro' I do try to come off like a high school kid having fun," he said. "What would a junior in high school say? What would their slang be? They use the word 'savage,' they use the word 'lit.' That isn't my personal vocabulary. But it comes out on camera."

The morning calm doesn't last long. The YouTube channels demand fresh content, and by 10 a.m. the team and its dewy-cheeked cameramen piled into a convoy of sport utility vehicles and headed off to the gym.

"Dude, I'm still picking glass out of my cheeks," said Chad Tepper, the unofficial masochist of Team 10, gingerly stroking his face as he rode in the back seat of Mr. Paul's tricked-out Tesla X. Holding out his phone, Mr. Tepper showed off footage from the previous day, a stunt filmed by an ultra-slow-motion Phantom camera showing a fluorescent light tube crashing down over his shoulder, enveloping his head — very, very slowly — in a cloud of glass shards and noxious white dust.

Such stunts might look like spontaneous iPhone goofs, but it often takes eight hours of shooting to create enough material for a 10-minute video. At that day's morning workout, for instance, an hour of sweat yielded 26 seconds of usable footage. Next, the team headed to a Ralphs supermarket on Sunset Boulevard, where they roamed the aisles brainstorming other stunts.

"Yo, what about just pouring milk into cereal?" Mr. Paul asked the group, his eyes partly hidden by his trademark "yellers," or yellow aviator sunglasses.

Too dull.

"We need to do something where we light something on fire," one team member said.

An hour later, the crew assembled at a parking lot and giddily began emptying their grocery bags. As the Phantom camera rolled, team members swatted a cup of Jell-O with a tennis racket, blasted Mr. Tepper in the face with mini-marshmallows fired from a T-shirt gun and dropped an egg onto the blades of a drone hovering at shoulder level, splattering several members of the team with an al dente aeronautic omelet as they doubled over in laughter.

For the pièce de résistance, Mr. Paul attempted a fire-breathing stunt involving dish soap, butane and cornstarch. Over Mr. Tepper's firm warnings ("Dude, I'm serious"), a cameraman ignited a puff of flammable foam in Mr. Paul's palm. The Team 10 leader then blew a pillow-size fire ball into the warm Hollywood air, then turned to the camera triumphantly, squawking, "I'm a dragon!" as he flapped his arms melodramatically, cornstarch cascading from his mouth.

"A lot of people get this awesome feeling when they go to a club, or they're out with their friends every night having fun," he said later. "But the feeling for me is freedom. Like, I can literally do whatever I want, whenever I want."

That has proved a blessing and a curse.

His overnight transformation into a rap star, for example, was a breakthrough moment, but it also made him, to some, hater bait of Vanilla Ice proportions.

It wasn't just the parody videos that were blossoming online."Everyday Bro" ranked high on YouTube's list of most-disliked videos (it's currently No. 7; Justin Bieber's "Baby" is No. 1), and the backlash dragged Mr. Paul into a series of highly publicized skirmishes with both intimates and rival YouTube stars.

Most prominent was the slugfest with his brother, Logan. The siblings traded menacing YouTube "diss tracks" over the song that were viewed hundreds of millions of times, each one solemnly dissected by teen magazines and gossip sites, as if they were nuclear threats between Donald Trump and Kim Jong-un.

At the same time, Mr. Paul was engaged in a high-traffic war of words with Alissa Violet, a former girlfriend and Team 10 protégée, which was quickly turning into a YouTube version of "All My Children," with allegations of cheating, emotional abuse and betrayal.

By July, with the neighborhood battle raging, Disney had apparently decided that Mr. Paul had become too hot to handle and announced that it had "mutually agreed" to part ways with its star.

To Mr. Paul, the point was becoming clear: As a budding captain of industry, he might have to learn to steer the Team 10 ship through the ice fields without ramming every last iceberg.

"All I can do is control myself," he said.

Following the fire-breathing stunt, Mr. Paul's grueling day was far from done. Around 8 p.m. he gathered the crew around the kitchen table for the weekly Team 10 meeting.

"First of all, we hit 80 million," Mr. Paul announced, gesturing toward a flat-screen television glowing orange with a graphic that read "80,095,981," Team 10's current subscriber base. "And we're also doubling the Kardashians in monthly growth." Team members, many wearing Team 10 hoodies and T-shirts, erupted in applause.

"I really think in the next six months, we can triple that, if not quadruple that," he said. "It's about coming together and pushing your boundaries every single day."

Afterward, Mr. Paul retreated to the only quiet place he could find — his Tesla, charging in the garage — to discuss his tumultuous summer. He seemed contrite. As was obvious to any Jake Pauler, he was making a big effort of late to atone for his perceived sins, to stress the positives of the Team 10 mission.

He had uploaded an apology confessional in which he talked about the difficulties of coming of age in the public eye with few mentors, a mea culpa rap song ("Pressure hard, they all watchin now, make a mistake, world on me now"), and a hug-and-make-up rap duet with Logan, "I Love You Bro," which has received 61 million views.

("Jake Paul apology raps are my new favorite genre of music," Seth Rogen said on Twitter.)

JAKE MICHAELS FOR THE NEW YORK TIMES

From left, Nathan Speiser, Mr. Paul and John Massey, strolling the aisles of Ralphs.

A week later, he would lead Team 10 off to hurricane-ravaged Houston, where they bought Sea-Doo water scooters and filmed themselves patrolling the flooded streets to rescue stranded storm victims and animals. Team 10 fund-raisers brought in about $150,000, he said.

To appease neighbors, he has toned down the noise and high jinks and, under a threat of arrest, has agreed not to shoot at the house without a permit. He was even promising to move, going on an aggressive house hunt for secluded quarters on the outskirts of Los Angeles.

"The people who are really close to me would walk in here and tell you that I'm a great person and that I've done nothing but good for them in their lives," Mr. Paul said. "But I can't be like, 'Hey, I'm a good person,' because no one cares. Anyone can say they're a good person."

Then again, what is hate, really, but just more content?

Later that evening, Mr. Paul headed back to the studio to answer his critics in the best way he knows how, a new rap video. Channeling

Eminem in “8 Mile,” he cut a feisty track in which he owned up to seemingly every last insult the haters had hurled at him.

“Fake wife, fake life, no talent at all,” he rapped. “Let me tell y’all about all of his flaws.”

“Sometimes I wanna quit it all, sometimes I wish I wasn’t involved, sometimes I wish I could hate Jake Paul.”

It is safe to assume that impulse passed.

As of this week, the video had attracted almost 25 million views.

Unboxing the Internet for Teens, Eightysomethings and Everyone in Between

BY AMANDA HESS | NOV. 21, 2017

SOMETIMES WHEN I tell people I write about internet culture for The New York Times, they look at me like I just said that I cover prom trends for "AARP The Magazine."

I get it. Our paper is known as "The Gray Lady," a nickname she shares with several famous ghosts. Part of my job is to help keep her relevant to the world of the living.

My semiofficial title at the paper is "Internet Critic," which means that I think about things like memes the same way other people think about movies or modern art. I also think a lot about how to talk about the internet in a 166-year-old newspaper. The Times has a vast and diverse audience, which means that when I write about a Snapchat filter, I'm writing about it for Snap addicts and for people who have never opened Snapchat in their lives.

I land somewhere between those two groups. I'm 32, and I'm neither a kid nor a parent. I try to strike a balance. I want my stories to be accessible to my most dedicated reader — my 89-year-old grandfather (Hi, Grandpa Jack!) — without turning away a 19-year-old reader who has never thought of The New York Times as a publication that's particularly relevant to her. (Maybe because The Times has not always thought much about catering to her interests.)

I came to internet culture a little bit sideways: Before I landed at The Times, I wrote about sex and gender for about 10 years, but I was always most interested in writing about the ways in which technology was upending those things, whether that meant the proliferation of queer One Direction fan fiction or the rise of the online harassment of women. I came to The Times last year as part of its inaugural David

Carr fellowship, which is dedicated to bringing young(er) writers into the paper to help carry on Mr. Carr's legacy of speaking truth to power while writing with personality and style.

Now that I'm here, I find that seemingly tiny details and tonal choices can have a big impact over how a story is perceived. There may yet be Times readers out there, for instance, who don't know what #TBT stands for, and lack the internet-native reflex to just Google it. But if I explain what #TBT means in a piece, internet-savvy readers will see it as a big flashing sign that says: "THIS COLUMN ISN'T FOR YOU." So I leave it be.

The last thing anybody wants is for The New York Times to explain some meme to them. Insead I try to think a little deeper about what people are doing and sharing on the internet, draw connections to society and history and politics, and trust that those Times readers who are hearing about an online phenomenon for the first time are smart enough to catch up quick and read between the lines.

Lately, I've been experimenting with internet criticism that doesn't have to be read at all. The Times recently debuted a new video series called "Internetting With Amanda Hess." The five episodes cover everything from how political memes threaten the democratic process to how conspiracy theories have taken on the contours of the social web. Each is a 4-minute-ish tour through a kind of hyper version of internet browsing. And they're all made in a vertical format, so they mimic the look of (and are best viewed on) mobile devices.

Our working tagline, "Everything weird, wrong, and totally sad about internet culture," partly reflects my pessimistic mood about the internet lately, but also signals our interest in conflict and argument.

The best and scariest part of it is that this is all really new for The Times, and for me, too. Before this, I'd never made a video in my life. Now I'm acting as scriptwriter and voice-over artist and producer, though I'm still not quite sure what that is. My pal and confidant is the brilliant "Internetting" video editor Shane O'Neill, who also wrote and performs the series' theme song. (I have a theme song!) As a words person, it's been amazing to be able to collaborate with someone who thinks really deeply about the way things look and sound.

And while it's still a challenge to make something about the internet that might appeal to everybody on it, it's helpful to be able to work on a couple of tracks at the same time. While the voice-over lays out an argumentative essay about the internet, the visuals situate the viewer in a place and time and layer in inside jokes and references. Whether we're trying to shine light on some obscure corner of the internet, or to reframe a familiar one through a new perspective, it's a revelation and a relief to be able to show rather than tell.

Facebook's Version of YouTube Takes Shape With Pranksters, Magicians and Cartoons

BY SAPNA MAHESHWARI | DEC. 16, 2018

The tech giant sees Facebook Watch, with its rising number of videos from internet stars, as a key to future growth.

A 20-SOMETHING MAGICIAN performing on the streets of Thailand and Jamaica. Three Australian brothers who shock bystanders with devious pranks. A conservative commentator in Mississippi who rants about America's priorities from his car.

These are some of the video makers who in recent months have started making serious money from Facebook Watch, the tech giant's answer to YouTube. Julius Dein, the magician, said his videos had attracted revenue in the "six figures" since July, when he became able to run ads on them. The prankster brothers, known as the Jalals, said they had earned more than $500,000 since August.

While Facebook grapples with growing regulatory scrutiny and a string of crises around data misuse on its platform, its ambitious growth plans have not slowed. The company's revenue, which now tops $40 billion a year, has increased by more than 30 percent every quarter since it went public in 2012. The tech giant has acknowledged that growth will slow over the next few years. So siphoning some of the more than $60 billion in advertising money that's now directed toward TV and bringing it to Watch has become a central goal.

But creating a space that can attract that money has been a challenge for Facebook. Since beginning Watch in August 2017, the company had limited the number of pages that could run video ads to a tightly curated set of entities, including well-known publishers, TV networks and celebrities like Jada Pinkett Smith and Tom Brady.

That has now changed. At the end of August, Facebook started to allow more pages to run ads on videos that were at least three minutes long. The number of Facebook pages that can run video ads has gone from about 3,700 on Aug. 1 to more than 23,000 this month, according to data shared with The New York Times by OpenSlate, an analytics firm that helps advertisers assess online video content.

While Facebook has invested in plenty of original programming and established shows like "Buffy the Vampire Slayer" this year, it has also opened up Watch to much more do-it-yourself content from comedians, video bloggers and other digital entertainers. In other words, the YouTube crowd — though the number of videos on Watch is a small fraction what's available on YouTube.

"They need premium, hit, intellectual-property-driven stuff to fuel the idea that this is TV-style content," said Ben Lerer, the chief executive of Group Nine Media, which oversees brands with popular Watch shows like "The Dodo" and "NowThis." "But then they need the volume that comes from News Feed content coming into Watch. That's a balance that's really delicate."

With more pages showing video ads, there are more places for advertisers to run their messages, and more opportunities for Facebook users to get access to videos on the platform.

Among the most popular of these pages are entries from mainstream companies like Disney, BuzzFeed and Vice, according to OpenSlate. But in October and December, the most popular pages included a provocative group of bare-chested performers known as Magic Men Live, and others with names like "Insane Stunts," "Jesus Today" and "Nurse Blake." There was little in the way of news and politics.

Facebook said on Thursday that more than 75 million people around the world spent at least one minute on Watch every day, and that those users then spent at least 20 minutes there on average. Ms. Pinkett Smith's "Red Table Talk" is its most-followed show and has the most active Facebook group, according to the company.

Fidji Simo, who leads Facebook's video efforts, said that most users were getting access to Watch by clicking into it from the platform's main site rather than through videos on their News Feed.

"Seeing how many people are coming in and watching for an average of more than 20 minutes has definitely been encouraging," Ms. Simo said. "We're really seeing this content create communities and social engagement on the platform."

When advertisers buy the commercials that appear before or during longer videos, they don't know if users are specifically in the Watch section of the site or if they're seeing the video in their News Feed, sandwiched between updates and photos from friends and family. For some, the distinction is important.

"One's a more lean-forward experience, and one's a more lean-back experience," said George Manas, who leads performance marketing across Omnicom Media Group agencies. "We're concerned that because it's running across both environments, it's creating challenges in measurement and, frankly, just in quality control because the user experience just isn't the same."

Graham Allen, the 31-year-old host of "Rant Nation With Graham Allen," a Watch show from Conservative Review's CRTV (which recently merged with TheBlaze to form Blaze Media), said the viewership had made up for a sharp drop in traffic to his personal page after Facebook shifted its algorithms to favor its video offering.

"Most people don't even realize that the majority of videos they're watching now on their News Feeds are from Watch pages," Mr. Allen said. "I don't know if that was intentional from Facebook, to make it a seamless transition, or they just didn't think it through enough, like, 'Wow, people might not be able to know the difference.' "

He added, "As far as video content goes, if you don't have a Watch page, you're kind of dead in the water right this second." The ad revenue has been welcome, he said, noting that he was previously more reliant on outside deals with sponsors.

Mr. Dein, a 24-year-old magician from London who posts videos of street performances around the world, was able to start running video ads on his page in July. He said Facebook's rules affected the kind of videos that performed well, noting that ads can run after a minute as long as the video is at least three minutes long.

"With me, since I'm magic, I'll make sure the ad is on an exciting moment of the video," Mr. Dein said. "If I'm about to cut my finger open for a magic trick, the ad plays just as the knife goes down."

Mr. Dein said he had found it harder to produce "super-viral videos," like one he posted last year about homeless people reacting to magic, which he said had been watched more than 200 million times. But he said it made sense for Facebook to mimic YouTube and adopt longer-form content to appeal to advertisers.

"If someone's watching a vlogger like Logan Paul and tuned into that person, they're paying more attention to the ad, whereas if someone is watching a seven-second clip, they don't care about the video or the ad," he said.

Max, Rebeen and Arman Jalal, who live in Melbourne, Australia, have amassed millions of fans on Facebook and YouTube through their unique and sometimes shocking brand of prank videos. (The brothers were once arrested after faking a series of terror attacks.)

The Jalals, who are in their late teens and early 20s, have been able to run ads on some of their videos since August, they said in a Skype interview. One Watch video that they posted in September, featuring a nun frightening people in places like a parking garage, attracted more than 130 million views and earned the brothers $140,000, they said.

While the data from OpenSlate data shows little news content among the most popular Watch videos, Ms. Simo said that was not a "deliberate strategy."

"News content tends to be on the shorter side, so we've seen a lot of news partners have a lot of one-minute videos," she said. Advertisers are also able to opt out of categories that tend to be closely related to news and politics, like "debated social issues" and "tragedy and conflict," she said.

THE MOST POPULAR PAGES WITH COMMERCIALS IN DECEMBER

1. The Lion King
2. Disney Off the Page
3. Bae or Bail
4. Little but Fierce
5. The Daily Goalcast
6. Born Different
7. Newsner.com
8. CHEESE INSIDER
9. Shammi
10. PixarToyStory
11. Andrea Espada
12. Blossom
13. Dear Alyne
14. Newsner Italia
15. Chester Tagg

Mark Zuckerberg, Facebook's chief executive, said on an October earnings call that Watch had "really hit its stride." Still, it's not yet a hot commodity among ad buyers.

Mr. Manas of Omnicom said that while the service had potential, advertisers were still figuring out how people react to ad breaks in social videos. The agency also wants more control over choosing the specific videos for its clients' ads, rather than simply being offered genres or other bundles.

Advertisers are also already spending plenty of money with Facebook on display ads and even other video ads, including sponsored posts that appear on the News Feed, said Susan Schiekofer, chief digital investment officer at GroupM, the media buying arm of ad giant WPP.

There are also numerous other online platforms offering original content, from Amazon, Netflix and Hulu to Snap and Google.

“The burden of proof is on Facebook’s end to be able to illustrate to people that they are providing a longer-form video experience,” Amanda Grant, GroupM’s United States head of paid social, said.

Still, Facebook has sought to learn from the mistakes of YouTube, which saw advertisers flee last year when their messages were found on videos promoting racism and terrorism. Facebook has sought to vet the pages that can introduce video ad breaks — the art of “brand safety,” as the industry calls it. OpenSlate, which helps brands with their YouTube ads, also recently introduced a product for Facebook that gives advertisers more control over which videos feature their ads.

“There’s a role for the highly produced content, but it’s more of the sizzle, not the steak,” said Mike Henry, the chief executive of OpenSlate. “Success for these guys will come from scale and diversity of content.”

“If Facebook gets this right and can generate scale of inventory and scale of audience, they have the opportunity to combine sight, sound and motion with incredible user targeting,” he said. “And that’s the holy grail.”

SAPNA MAHESHWARI covers advertising. She has won reporting awards from the Society of American Business Editors and Writers and the Newswomen’s Club of New York and was on Time’s list of “140 Best Twitter Feeds of 2014.”

Online and Making Thousands, at Age 4: Meet the Kidfluencers

BY SAPNA MAHESHWARI | MARCH 1, 2019

Brands are giving lucrative endorsement deals to young children on YouTube and Instagram, raising questions about whether their young followers should be seeing that kind of marketing.

SAMIA WAS AN influencer before she could talk.

Her parents, Adam and LaToya Ali, are influencers themselves and began chronicling Samia's impending arrival on YouTube and Instagram in 2014, once Ms. Ali learned she was pregnant.

"Samia's birth video is on YouTube, so she's pretty much been born into social media," Mr. Ali said.

Samia is now 4 and has 143,000 followers on Instagram and 203,000 subscribers on YouTube. Her feeds are mostly populated with posts of her posing and playing, but they also feature paid promotions for brands like Crayola and HomeStyle Harvest chicken nuggets.

There are instances when "Samia can't verbatim get the message out," Mr. Ali, who lives in the Atlanta area, said of the promotional posts. "Sometimes, their talking points are not kid talk, so LaToya would need to appear, or myself, to relay those because those are key deliverables that the brands want."

Welcome to the world of kidfluencers. Brands have flocked to influencers — individuals, famous or not, with large followings on social media — for years, hoping their online popularity will prompt their fans to buy the products they vouch for. Then child influencers started appearing on their parents' profiles, a surreal but seemingly harmless offshoot of this phenomenon.

Now, advertisers like Walmart, Staples and Mattel are bankrolling lucrative endorsements deals for toddlers and tweens with large followings and their own verified profiles on YouTube and Instagram.

AUDRA MELTON FOR THE NEW YORK TIMES

Samia Ali, 4, getting help shooting a YouTube video, "How to Be a Good Kid," in front of her parents, LaToya and Adam, in their home near Atlanta.

As a result, children too young to make their own accounts on the platforms are being turned into tastemakers.

Instagram, owned by Facebook, and YouTube, which is part of Google, are designed for adults in large part because of a federal privacy law that protects children under 13. Bios for many of the younger influencers on Instagram note that the pages are "run by parents," and YouTube channels are presumably registered to their guardians.

Because they say their platforms are 13-and-older zones, technology companies do not have to comply with federal rules that limit targeted advertising and data collection. But Josh Golin, executive director of the Campaign for a Commercial-Free Childhood, said the companies had no incentive to keep children off the sites.

And as TV ratings continue to fall and children spend more time online, advertisers are spending more money to reach them there.

"The fact that brands are using actual children as influencers is a very clear sign that they're targeting children that they know are on these platforms," Mr. Golin said.

That can mean big money for the families of kidfluencers. Kyler Fisher, the father of 2-year-old identical twins who have more than two million followers on Instagram, said a sponsored post on the girls' account could fetch between $10,000 and $20,000.

The twins, Taytum and Oakley, have promoted car seats and Carnival Cruise Lines on Instagram. They are also central to the success of their parents' YouTube channel, Kyler & Mad, which has about three million subscribers. Promotions on the family YouTube channel can draw $25,000 to $50,000.

Fans are so interested in the family that their third child, due the first week of March, already has 112,000 Instagram followers.

"My kids complete the package, man," Mr. Fisher said. "If we didn't have the girls, I can't imagine being as far as we are."

Another parent shared the prices commanded by the parent's child on the condition of anonymity, citing concern that the disclosures could harm negotiations with brands. The parent said brands might pay $10,000 to $15,000 for a promotional Instagram post while a sponsored YouTube video might earn $45,000. A 30- to 90-second shout-out in a longer video can cost advertisers between $15,000 and $25,000.

Brands are also pursuing children with smaller followings. The toy company Melissa & Doug emailed parents about a six-week influencer campaign last summer, offering payments and free toys for weekly Instagram posts of their children "having fun with the toys!" The company said it would pay $10 per 1,000 followers for individual Instagram posts and $5 per 1,000 followers for Instagram Story posts.

The rise of this kind of advertising has raised questions involving fair compensation, oversight and work permits, especially since child labor guidelines vary by state.

Andrea Faville, a YouTube spokeswoman, said that the site didn't allow anyone under 13 to make or own accounts and that it worked "closely with experts, nonprofit organizations and others in our industry to protect families using our services."

YouTube came under fire last month after lewd comments by pedophiles were discovered on innocent videos of children; the company has since said it will suspend comments on most videos of minors. Some channels that can "demonstrate a low risk of predatory behavior" will keep comments but require moderators, the company said. It remains to be seen if disabling comments will hurt the kind of connections kidfluencers try to establish with their fans.

Sravanthi Dev, a spokeswoman for Instagram, said that while the platform prohibited users 12 and under, their parents or representatives could create profiles for them "as long as it is clear in the bio information that the account is run by the parent or representative."

Michelle Foley's 6-year-old daughter, Ava, and her best friend, Everleigh, also 6, have more than a million followers on their shared Instagram and YouTube accounts. YouTube's analytics say Ava and Everleigh's viewers are largely between the ages of 25 and 44, Ms. Foley said, but she said she thought the core audience was between 8 and 18.

"When we go out, parents never know who we are, but kids do," Ms. Foley said.

Alex Chavez-Munoz, a founder of Viral Talent, which works with child influencers, also disputed the data.

"When you see the analytics of a kidfluencer channel, the dominant audience is 25- to 34-year-old women," Mr. Chavez-Munoz said. "That's obviously not the case. The case is that the child is watching it on their parents' device."

In December, a 9-year-old kidfluencer known as Txunamy shared a photo on Instagram and asked her more than two million followers to comment on it and share their ages. Thousands of replies flooded in: 9, 10, 11 years old.

Captiv8, which connects brands with influencers, found more than 3,100 Instagram influencers, from a sample of 1.2 million accounts, who are likely under 13 based on terms in their bios like "managed by mom." (Instagram has more than a billion users.) Each account had at least 1,000 followers.

On YouTube, the much bigger kid influencer destination, there are toy accounts like Ryan ToysReview, whose young star earned $22 million in a year, according to Forbes. But children, under their parents' watch, are also building followings on YouTube and Instagram as gamers, video bloggers, fashionistas, mischievous toddlers and personalities who anchor family channels, which are often a cross between reality TV, pranks and random skits. YouTube accounts can also bring in serious ad dollars without brand deals, which are shared with the site.

Everleigh's grandmother, whom Ms. Foley met when they worked together, came up with the idea of making an Instagram account for the girls when they were 10 months old, calling them "besties" and dressing them in matching outfits. The girls went "viral" eight months later after the account helped them land a modeling campaign for the Kardashian Kids line, Ms. Foley said.

At that point, "we were like, 'We should start a YouTube,' but they couldn't talk," she said. "So then we kind of waited for them to start talking."

The girls also have their own separate Instagram accounts. Everleigh's sponsored posts have included promotions for toys ("I'm excited to share that the new PAW Patrol Mighty Pups line is available exclusively at Walmart!") and Disney dolls ("Everleigh is in LOVE with her Fancy Nancy dolls!").

The girls have made celebrities out of the rest of their families. Ava's 1-year-old brother has 148,000 Instagram followers, and Everleigh's newborn sister has a million. Recently, Everleigh started a YouTube channel, Everleigh Opens Toys, and Ava is interested in making one, too, Ms. Foley said.

"If it wasn't for Everleigh and Ava, I would not have what I have today," she said.

Brands want to team up with children for the same reasons they want to work with older social media personalities — their follower counts, the ability to post more quickly than traditional ad agencies, the way the posts feel like recommendations from a friend. But advocates say these techniques can deceive children, who are in the early stages of understanding and recognizing advertisements.

Children's television, overseen by the Federal Communications Commission, has rules that separate ads from content and limit product placement and promotions by a program's host or characters. The internet doesn't.

YouTube has its own guidelines for children's advertising, but they are often hard to police. For example, the YouTube Kids app, designed for children 12 and under, is not supposed to contain sponsored content, but The New York Times found several paid advertorial videos from influencers there for companies like Walmart, Dreamworks and Claire's. (YouTube removed the videos after The Times asked about them.)

"It is very manipulative of young children," said Kathryn Montgomery, a professor emerita at American University's School of Communications. "With this form of promotion and advertising, there is a purposeful blurring of those lines."

Ava and Everleigh's YouTube channel peppers sponsored videos among dance battles and hangouts with other influencers. Ms. Foley said the family could get 10 email requests a day from brands.

The girls posted a 10-minute sponsored video for Mattel in November titled "First Sleepover Opening Giant Presents!" An adult asked the children, clad in matching pajamas, about their holiday wish list, which was "Barbie everything!" They appeared to sleep, then woke up, squealing, to wrapped Barbie merchandise.

Mattel declined to comment on its child influencer strategy.

In an advertorial video for Staples, Txunamy declared her excitement about back-to-school shopping at the chain, then showcased her "haul."

"Whenever we work with younger influencers, all contracts and negotiations are conducted through their parents or talent agencies directly representing them," said Meghan McCarrick, a spokeswoman for Staples.

Social media stars aren't typically considered actors under the law. In California, a portion of child actors' earnings are set aside in a trust based on the decades-old Coogan Law, named for a former child star whose parents spent all his money by the time he turned 21. Similar trusts are required by New York, Louisiana and New Mexico. For kid-fluencers, it's usually a voluntary decision by parents to create these accounts.

Several families said they had established the accounts after working on traditional TV shows or national commercials.

As for the children, it can be tough for them to understand how much of a fuss they're creating.

Samia's father, Mr. Ali, said, "She doesn't have a concept of viral or 'views,' so it's almost like, for her, walking into an experiment to learn something — it's more of us giving her a task or assignment, where she has something to conquer."

He added, "We'll know when she gets a sense of her following and let her know what this all means."

SAPNA MAHESHWARI covers advertising. She has won reporting awards from the Society of American Business Editors and Writers and the Newswomen's Club of New York and was on Time's list of "140 Best Twitter Feeds of 2014."

CHAPTER 2

Just Who Influences Who?

Just who are influencers? They run the gamut from thrill seekers, actors, comedians, musicians, models — even cats. They're all chasing one thing: followers. Having millions of followers allows social media influencers to cash in on sponsorships and advertising dollars when they promote businesses to their audience. Gatherings like VidCon allow burgeoning celebrities to meet their fans and encourage others to learn the digital ropes.

ILoveMakonnen Is Big Online and Almost Famous

BY JOE COSCARELLI | APRIL 4, 2015

WAITING FOR THE real world to catch up to Internet fame can be awkward, especially for a digital native accustomed to a daily cascade of favorites, retweets, streams and followers. Just ask ILoveMakonnen, the 25-year-old singer and rapper from Atlanta (best known as simply Makonnen), whose video for the hit single "Tuesday," featuring Drake, has been seen more than 73 million times on YouTube.

Last month, at the South by Southwest music festival, that buzz was more than enough to get Makonnen into the V.I.P. area of an after-hours party and to have him recognized by a female fan — but one who had not yet mastered his name. "MACK-a-nin!" she shouted repeatedly from behind a barricade. (It's Muh-KO-nen.) He leaned in for a hug before skeptically eying his handler and disappearing back through the crowd.

"You don't even know my name!" Makonnen, born Makonnen Sheran, said the following week, recalling the run-in. "You're just yelling because of Drake. If you really know my music, you're going to know how to say my name. I say it all the damn time."

This is the in-between space where Makonnen resides: recognizable — as the teddy bear with a rich crown of curls, seen by millions on Twitter, Instagram and Snapchat — but still not quite famous after a year that included a Grammy nomination and a performance on "The Tonight Show Starring Jimmy Fallon" (both for "Tuesday," a spacey anthem for weekday partyers).

On Tuesday, he released the fifth installment in his "Drink More Water" mixtape series, and this month he will set out on his first headlining tour, followed by a slate of summer festivals, ahead of his debut full-length album, due out by year's end on Drake's OVO Sound, an imprint of Warner Bros. Records. (Shows at the Bowery Ballroom, on April 28, and the Music Hall of Williamsburg, on April 29, have already sold out.)

But Makonnen is also a wild card and an oddball, even for the New Weird Atlanta rap scene with which he is often associated as the city churns out eccentric stars like the robot crooner Future, the mantra-chanting trio Migos and the yelping alien Young Thug.

While Makonnen also trades on the singularity of his voice — a gooey Broadway baritone that he can stretch into a squeal — and works with the same trap music producers that built the city's current opulent drug-den sound, he is barely a rapper at all, splitting the difference between singers like Morrissey and Nate Dogg, and drawing equally from his favorite rock bands, like the Killers, and the Atlanta rap kingmaker Gucci Mane. On "Drink More Water 5," Makonnen switches easily between tough, club-ready songs about dealing drugs or ducking the police and the drumless, melancholic wail of solo piano numbers like "Get Loose With Me."

AN RONG XU FOR THE NEW YORK TIMES

The singer and rapper ILoveMakonnen, also known as Makonnen, in the East Village last month. He has a gooey Broadway baritone that he can stretch into a squeal and is barely a rapper at all.

"I identify with the Internet more than New Atlanta," Makonnen said during a break from recording at Red Bull Studios in Manhattan, not far from his newly rented Chelsea apartment. He was at ease in a tie-dye T-shirt that combined the logos for Versace, Gucci, Louis Vuitton and Chanel, with heavy eyelids from a recent smoking session. "I didn't come out of Atlanta like that, where I was beating up the streets and doing a whole bunch of shows or mixtape after mixtape. I was doing my own thing online."

That was mostly by necessity. The day after his high school graduation, Makonnen, then 18, witnessed the death of his best friend when a gun the two were messing with in a parked car discharged, striking the other teenager in the head. Although the shooting was initially ruled an accident, Makonnen was later arrested and charged with involuntary manslaughter after the victim's mother encouraged further investigation, he said.

The two had planned to attend the Air Force Academy using the "buddy program" to be stationed together. "We were that close of friends," Makonnen said, remembering sleepovers and trips to church together. "It was a tragedy."

Makonnen would spend the next seven years under state supervision, first in an ankle monitor while awaiting trial, and then, after a plea deal, on probation. Keeping him busy and sane throughout that period, he said, were two pit bulls, Daisy and Snow, "the Internet and my keyboard," an earlier gift from his mother, who had hoped that learning piano would keep him inside and out of trouble.

His old Gateway desktop computer, especially, was a window to the outside world. "I would stay up all night," Makonnen said. "Everybody's always up on the Internet."

He became obsessed with MP3 sites and Myspace, before starting his own blog, The Newness, where he posted movie trailers, fantasized about exotic locales and interviewed anyone who would respond to his online messages. They included the rapper Lil B — a spiritual father to ILoveMakonnen, whose hundreds of songs also tend to be one-take stream-of-consciousness sketches — and the chief executive of Zappos.com, Tony Hsieh.

"I used to be such a geek," Makonnen said.

In addition to growing his online network, Makonnen was self-producing music for him and his mother to sing over, recording multiple bedroom albums influenced by synth bands like MGMT and Bloc Party. While on probation, Makonnen also attended cosmetology classes, where he specialized in coloring hair and dreamed of styling for "runways in Milan or Paris and Vogue fashion shoots," he said. "I was just around girls all day. I really became a girl — I learned so much about them."

His songs today feature specific female characters and experiences, and a beauty school mannequin head he calls Martha has become an aesthetic trademark. Although Makonnen knows his interests may be considered outré in rap, he laughs at his reputation as a weirdo with the self-assuredness of someone used to sticking out.

But having moved to the mostly black Riverdale section of Atlanta from Los Angeles at 13, Makonnen was also fluent in the language of hip-hop. In high school, "I just hung around hustlers," selling drugs and fake designer purses for pocket money, he said.

Combining these experiences with an indie-rock sensibility and D.I.Y. work ethic caught the attention of Atlanta's burgeoning producer class, including Mike Will Made-It, who has worked with Rihanna and Miley Cyrus. He signed Makonnen to a publishing deal with Warner Bros. in 2013.

But it wasn't until Makonnen linked with the next-generation beatmakers — and "Tuesday" co-architects — Sonny Digital and Metro Boomin the next year that his sound started to coalesce. "They liked my tone of voice," Makonnen said.

Sonny Digital (real name Sonny Uwaezuoke) said he first learned of Makonnen online and did not know initially that he was based in Atlanta. "It sounded funny at first — it was just him and his keyboard," Sonny Digital said. "But Makonnen opened up the doors for us to do something different. What 'Tuesday' really did for all of us was give us room to be a little more creative and new, to show people that we're not just confined to doing hard trap music."

Makonnen, fresh off probation, had also recently discovered hallucinogenic drugs, which he credits with "unlocking" his mind, and he said he was tripping on mushrooms and frustrated from a long night in the studio when he first heard that Drake had added a verse to his song — a ticket to ride in rap today.

"I cried," Makonnen said of the moment last August, which was captured on video and went viral. "Tuesday" exploded on radio and hit No. 12 on the Billboard Hot 100.

But while his induction into that tastemaking Toronto rapper's extended crew was like winning the music lottery, it's not an endgame. "I'm not trying to be in hip-hop and rap, really," Makonnen said. "It's so sad, but I just knew that was the way for me to get in, because I'm 'black' and I'm 'urban' and I'm from Atlanta."

"The rap world thinks I'm gay," he said. "A lot of people out there do. They think I'm a homosexual, which is not a problem. I don't want to say I'm gay, I'm straight, I'm bisexual or any of that, because that's just. …" he said, trailing off. "Who cares? All that's doing is dividing us."

By using today's hot regional sound to acquaint audiences with his theatrical voice and stylistic quirks, Makonnen hopes to ride with "the kids and the Internet" on a new wave, one he likens aesthetically to "a cross between Valentine's Day and Halloween." Already, his latest mixtape uses street raps as a Trojan horse for '80s-influenced piano ballads and psychedelic electropop.

"What you do is, you hook them on the drug, and then you start switching the drug," Makonnen said. "And then they like it."

Drizzy and the New Celebrity Worship

BY JENNA WORTHAM | MAY 28, 2015

A FEW WEEKS AGO, I messaged a friend to ask how her film project was going. She replied, "Always felt like my vision been bigger than the bigger picture." Then, a few days later, after filling me in on her summer plans, she sent another non sequitur: "I am on a 24-hour Champagne diet!!!" Eventually, she confessed that she was using an app called Drizzy, which lets users send text messages made of snippets of the rapper Drake's lyrics. Such a service might sound limited in its appeal, but that hasn't stopped half a million people from downloading the app since it was released in March; right after it was released, so many people were searching and texting Drake lyrics that the server crashed. It's just one of several dozen apps that exist only to help smartphone users relish in and broadcast their love of Drake.

A couple of decades earlier, all these people might have instead been inundating Drake's fan club headquarters with self-addressed stamped envelopes, hoping for an autographed headshot. But celebrity fandom has migrated, quite happily, from lockers and bedroom walls to our smartphones — and into the grown-up world more broadly. Kim Kardashian: Hollywood, the reality star's mobile gaming app, made headlines for raking in tens of millions of dollars, but the world of app-based celebrity worship goes much deeper. There's the BeyHive, an ad hoc social network for Beyoncé fans. There are photo booth apps that let fans "pose" with their favorite artists, like One Direction or Nicki Minaj. There's even Flying Cyrus, a riff on the game Flappy Bird; rather than flapping her wings, Miley wags her tongue. Reality stars have them (the cast of "RuPaul's Drag Race") and online celebrities do, too (a chubby Vine-famous boy named TerRio). Many of these apps are fan-made, but especially after the Kardashian success, celebrities increasingly want in on the action themselves. Britney Spears and Katy Perry recently announced plans to release their own mobile games.

Drake, despite all his Web-based popularity, seemed to shrug off the whole Internet in a recent song, saying, "Going online, that ain't part of my day." But that claim, like so many made in rap songs, sounds dubious: Not too long ago, an app called Drake Shake went viral. It allows users to add images of the rapper to photos. Soon after, Drake posted a photo of himself on Instagram, with his likeness pasted into the foreground. Clearly, he had been using Drake Shake, seemingly as susceptible to the appeal of fan apps as the rest of us.

At VidCon, Small-Screen Stars and Big-Time Fame

BY NICK BILTON | JULY 22, 2015

THEY SHOULD POST a sign in Anaheim, Calif., this week warning adults: "Keep out! Screaming teens everywhere."

On Thursday, more than 18,000 star-struck frenetic teenagers will descend on the Anaheim Convention Center for VidCon, a conference for online video makers, where they will spend three days running around like total and utter lunatics, all the while recording, editing and live-streaming on their mobile phones.

These teenagers will be on the hunt for celebrities with names like Smosh, Burnie Burns, TheThirdPew, Markiplier, Ksiolajidebt, Connor Franta, Flula Borg and Superwoman. To you and me, these monikers are completely unrecognizable. Yet to the kids in Anaheim, these people are more famous and important than any other mainstream A-list celebrity.

Feeling old and out of touch yet? I am. And don't worry, even people on the same stratosphere as these kids don't get half of what's going on.

"I've been to almost every major conference or fan event related to fandom, and never have I seen such mayhem and screaming that I have seen at VidCon," said Veronica Belmont, an online video personality and the host of "Dear Veronica," a show on Engadget.com. "Hotel lobbies are filled with flocks of teens that are like a force of nature, chasing after video stars that I have never even heard of before."

This is exactly why VidCon has become so important culturally. The conference was founded in 2010 by two brothers, Hank and John Green, of the VlogBrothers YouTube channel. They are, as the kids like to say, kind of a big deal; Hank interviewed President Obama recently on YouTube, and John is the author of "The Fault in Our Stars." In its short history, VidCon has become the barometer for just how quickly and fervently online video has changed.

"The generation that used to wait outside 1515 Broadway for MTV's 'TRL Live' to finish taping is now the same generation that will be waiting outside of the Hilton Anaheim for their YouTube stars to come out," said Casey Neistat, who is officially introducing his new video app, Beme, at the conference.

When VidCon began, there were 1,400 people in attendance, and almost all the video creators shared their shows on YouTube. Back then, most of those clips were viewed on a laptop. Now, five years later, the number of attendees has grown by 1,200 percent, and while YouTube is still insanely popular for video stars, clips are now created and watched on apps like YouNow, Snapchat, Periscope, Vine, Meerkat and Keek, not to mention new video features from Twitter, Facebook and Instagram.

For some people, all of these new apps and celebrities you've never heard of can feel overwhelming. But Hank Green sees the chaos and mayhem as a perfect indicator of why you don't need to be apprised of every little thing happening with online video.

"You have to think about this like each platform is its own genre," Mr. Green said in a phone interview. He likened the scads of video apps to the vast offerings on Netflix: There are thousands of options, and not everything will appeal to everyone, so users should only care about what they like. "It's O.K. to not know everything about everything in the world," he said.

The same applies once you go into the rabbit hole of each platform, where new shows often find their audiences through the proliferation of obscure, app-specific hashtags. Take #sleepingsquad, currently trending on the live-streaming app YouNow, which shows teenagers who film themselves sleeping for hours while onlookers watch and comment in real time.

Snapchat has thousands of bizarre little video trends, like ugly face contests, but these never reverberate outside a group of friends because nothing is posted to the Web. Another phenomenon, #SHTuesdays (Sexy Hips Tuesdays), highlights self-posted wacky videos of people dancing. That "show" is popular mostly on Vine, an app that will be representing in force at VidCon and that continues to mint new stars.

To put its reach into perspective, consider that one of Vine's biggest stars today, KingBach, has logged more than 4.5 billion views on the platform, where he plays a dramatic, almost cartoonlike caricature of himself. By comparison, Justin Bieber (who often appears in KingBach's videos) has been watched only 800,000,000 times on Vine.

Jason Mante, the head of user experience at Vine, said that these new stars have huge followings and will be chased after at VidCon because they spend so much time engaging with their audiences in a way that traditional stars do not. "When they post a new Vine, it's not just stuffing a story into six seconds, it's the next chapter or the next sentence of the larger story that they are telling," Mr. Mante said.

So if none of this makes any sense to you, don't fret. We now live in a world where your phone has become your television, and your apps have become the TV channels. Big stars are no longer created on big screens, but rather on smaller ones. And it's perfectly fine if you have no clue who they are.

Hollywood Rushes to VidCon to Connect With Millennials

BY BROOKS BARNES | MAY 22, 2016

LOS ANGELES — Ask movie marketers about the value of fan conventions, and their answer usually starts with an exhausted sigh. Between Comic-Con and WonderCon and Dragon Con, just to name a few, there are more cons than they need or want.

Well, add another one to the list: VidCon has become too big to ignore.

Founded six years ago in the basement of a hotel here, VidCon brings together online video creators and their fans. Last year, about 21,000 people — teenagers mostly — paid up to $150 each to see YouTube personalities like Bart Baker, attend panels ("The Family that Vlogs Together, Stays Together") and browse 600,000 square feet of exhibit space at the Anaheim Convention Center, where the annual event is now held.

The next VidCon, scheduled for June 23-25, will attract roughly 30,000 people, organizers say, and Hollywood will be there in a major way for the first time. New exhibitors and sponsors include 20th Century Fox, Netflix and Warner Bros., which is planning an elaborate stunt for "Fantastic Beasts and Where to Find Them," its Harry Potter prequel. Universal Pictures, which made a low-key VidCon debut last year, will return to screen "The Secret Life of Pets," a big-budget animated film.

Rather than just showing film clips, as it has done in years past, Lionsgate will raise the ante by bringing Emma Roberts, the star of "Nerve," a coming thriller. DreamWorks Animation has a promotion planned for "Trolls," which is set for release in November.

"Even if I wanted to fight against it, it would be like bailing out the Titanic," Hank Green, VidCon's co-founder, said of the Hollywood rush.

Other new non-entertainment VidCon sponsors include AOL, Calvin Klein, Hasbro, Marriott, Mars, NYX Cosmetics and Samsung.

Returning companies include Best Buy, Covergirl, Kia and Taco Bell. The convention's biggest sponsor, of course, is YouTube, which will bring in more than 200 representatives from top advertisers and try to connect them to video creators.

In many ways, VidCon is a younger version of Comic-Con International, the pop culture bacchanal attended by more than 130,000 people each summer in San Diego. Comic-Con has long been a powerful tool for movie and television marketers because it gives them one-stop access to Generation X fans. With its emphasis on YouTube personalities, VidCon serves up the millennial and postmillennial equivalent.

The VidCon audience, which tends to be more female than male, is one that "advertisers are finding more and more difficult to reach through traditional marketing channels," said Brent Weinstein, the head of digital media at United Talent Agency, which handles VidCon sponsorships. Television is losing its effect; millennials and postmillennials consume programming from video-on-demand services. In fact, studies have shown that this demographic tunes out anything that looks like a traditional ad, online or otherwise.

But they do pay attention to their Snapchat, Twitter and Facebook feeds. By placing a product — movie, lipstick, candy bar, doodad — directly in front of the socially voracious VidCon swarms, marketers can sometimes create meaningful digital chatter that stretches far beyond the convention hall.

"It's a chance for a direct conversation with a very important, hard-to-reach audience," said Blair Rich, Warner's executive vice president of worldwide movie marketing. Noting that many YouTube personalities have global followings, Ms. Rich added, "The VidCon influencers offer tremendous scale, and that really matters to us."

Along with "Fantastic Beasts," due in theaters in November, Warner will use the convention to promote "Lights Out," a coming thriller that started as a YouTube short.

Just as it took Hollywood years to hone its Comic-Con playbook, studios are still learning what works at VidCon.

Last year, spotting what it thought was a perfect opportunity for its low-budget "Jem and the Holograms," Universal ran a contest in which convention attendees could win cameo roles by making and sharing "Jem"-related videos. If the stunt attracted any attention, it certainly did not help the movie, which took in just $2.2 million at the box office.

Universal got a better result for "The Visit," a horror film that was screened at VidCon 2015. Attendees reacted with positive posts, which Universal then used to build additional interest a few weeks later at Comic-Con. "The Visit," directed by M. Night Shyamalan and costing $5 million to make, collected nearly $100 million worldwide.

"As an emerging event, VidCon can be a real accelerator for a certain type of movie," said Michael Moses, Universal's co-president of marketing.

Hollywood did not wake up to VidCon overnight. Television networks like Nickelodeon, NBC and HGTV were early adopters; Jeffrey Katzenberg, the departing chief executive of DreamWorks Animation, gave the convention's keynote address in 2014.

Still, the entertainment industry's more aggressive embrace is sudden enough that it could create a backlash among attendees, especially if VidCon's celebration of online video appears muddled as a result. Blistering growth — 359 panels are planned for June, up from 297 last year — inevitably gets messy.

Mr. Green, who founded VidCon with his brother, John Green, the author of "The Fault in Our Stars," said he ultimately views Hollywood's arrival as a positive development.

"The overlap is great, in part because it's important for studios to understand video fans and creators, both the culture and the excitement," he said. "That will hopefully lead to fewer studio efforts in this area that are inauthentic and gross."

Bo Burnham, Discovered on the Internet, Now Challenges It

BY JASON ZINOMAN | JUNE 3, 2016

IT'S BEEN A DECADE since Bo Burnham, then 16, uploaded a video of himself to a fairly new site called YouTube. He was singing a song about how his family thought he was gay.

After the video went viral and was seen by millions of viewers, he earned offers from Hollywood, a special on Comedy Central, a theater tour and a deal with Netflix. Bypassing the traditional route to stand-up success, Mr. Burnham grew into a boldly theatrical and formally clever comedian whose trailblazing career was a forceful defense of the internet as a comedy incubator. That's why it's startling that he has now emerged as one of its most scathing critics. It's as if the monster turned on Frankenstein.

"If you look at original content on YouTube now, the center of it is all-caps comments and girls' cleavage and commercial, derivative" videos aimed at "what 13-year-olds want rather than what they need," Mr. Burnham said Monday night in a Williamsburg apartment where he's staying while acting in a movie. "I don't mean to sound fatherly, but it's amazing to watch a medium sell out on steroids."

Citing the work of the author Douglas Rushkoff, Mr. Burnham said that watching the proliferation of comedy online had made him appreciate the virtue of old-fashioned gatekeepers. "I don't think democracy is a good thing always," he said. "This world of Rotten Tomatoes and user ratings on Amazon makes for safe, homogeneous choices. It's made me go: Studio executives aren't that bad."

There have been hints of this new-media skepticism in his work for years, from his underrated, short-lived MTV show, "Zach Stone Is Gonna Be Famous," which followed a fame-hungry teenager desperate to perform his life for the internet, to his more mature stand-up that uses disembodied voices and dramatic lighting to make him look and sound like a man trapped in his own art. But it wasn't until Mr. Burnham finished writing his third special, "Make Happy," which debuted on Netflix on Friday, that he decided to stop hinting and add a thesis statement of sorts.

"Social media is the market's answer to a generation that wanted to perform," he said toward the end of the hourlong special, crouching low to the ground, while describing the constant exhibitionism of online life as a prison. "I don't know anything about anything, but what I do know is if you can live without an audience, you should do it."

Mr. Burnham's comedy has always skewered pop culture (the new show takes aim at the faux populism of country music and the uplift of anthems like "Roar"), but what makes this special stand out is how it examines the shrinking distance between audience and performer in the internet era. "I want to talk about my relationship with the audience," he said. "I used to think I shouldn't because it's unreliable and stupid and 'poor me.' But I think people relate to this idea of having to perform something for people, the idea that the world around you is more of an audience than it used to be."

Comedians can be romantic about the response from their audience. Jerry Seinfeld famously claims that after several minutes, his fame has no influence on his act. Mr. Burnham finds that absurd, arguing that those comics are "desperately trying to act like they haven't lost that thing they love they had when they were younger — the 'I'm still struggling.' No, it's easier for you now," he said. "There's a huge desperate impulse from a lot of famous comedians to humanize themselves."

In his show, Mr. Burnham skewers Jimmy Fallon's "Tonight Show" celebrity lip-sync segments, which he calls the "end of culture." It's an example of the internet ethos bleeding into television. "It's the tearing down of the fake edifice of these people being better than us: multimillion-dollar beautiful people performing their own humanity for us in their $10,000 dresses," Mr. Burnham said. "I think comedy is destroyed when it gets in bed with celebrity."

As his argument about the corrosiveness of fame gains momentum, Mr. Burnham stands up, his thin but no longer lanky six-and-half-foot frame jittery with energy. Pointing out the hypocrisy of rich comedians talking about airport woes, when in reality they fly private, he said: "I want you to leave my show skeptical about performance."

In his special, Mr. Burnham adopts a prickly persona, establishing a tense relationship with his audience members, alternating between making them laugh and baiting, even insulting them. In part, this is rooted in a personal anxiety. Three years ago, Mr. Burnham, who considers himself a writer who fell into performance, started experiencing panic attacks before shows. This is reflected in how his special portrays the audience. "In comedy specials, the audience is always smiling and well lit," he said. "To me, they're a mob, faceless black entity. They are intimidating, strange and creepy."

At the end of the special, he thanks the crowd then says in a blankly affectless deadpan, "I hope you're happy." It is wonderfully teasing, grateful on the one hand, bitter on the other.

It may be the last thing a crowd will hear from him in a many years, since Mr. Burnham says he plans to take a long break from stand-up to focus on writing, get a movie about a middle schoolgirl off the ground and avoid the stage. He added that the demands on a comic these days mean that people send him tweets asking, "Are you dead?" after he's been working on a special for a few years. "A band can take a break but a comedian?" he said. "If you're not on '@midnight' every month you're Thomas Pynchon."

Mr. Burnham said he rejects the expectation of an "IV drip of entertainment." At the same time, he understands how his critique of online culture looks coming from him. "As someone who hugely benefited from it and maybe bears in part the guilt of what feels like an unfair advantage," he said, referring to his peculiar career path, which skipped the usual dues-paying steps, "I feel I need to expose what I know."

A Celebrity Z-List? Yes, It Exists

BY AMANDA HESS | AUG. 31, 2016

WHEN SOFIA RICHIE chopped her hair and visited a doctor's office recently, Us Weekly was there. Not to be outdone, People heralded Mindy McKnight as "the voice for millennial moms." And In Touch offered an "adorable" picture of Sarah Wright Olsen's infant napping next to a plush rabbit.

Meet the striving celebrity underclass that has risen to dominate the gossip machine. Aspiring models, third-tier reality show stars, impossible-to-place actors, YouTube vloggers and viral news subjects can now all curry coverage just by replenishing their social media accounts with photos of their babies, their butts or both. These are people you've probably never heard of — or have a nagging suspicion you might have, but don't quite know why.

For the record, Ms. Richie is a teenager best known for appearing on Justin Bieber's Instagram account (not to mention being Lionel Richie's daughter). Ms. McKnight films hair tutorials on YouTube. And because In Touch didn't bother to explain who Ms. Wright Olsen even is, I Googled it. Turns out that after a supporting role on the short-lived NBC sitcom "Marry Me," she now runs a parenting blog.

These quasi-celebrities have crept onto our radar through our supermarket tabloids and Facebook news feeds, and a crop of publications has emerged to cover them, whether sincerely or satirically. The relentless Instagram gossip outpost The Shade Room airs their dirty laundry, the deliciously absurd podcast "Who? Weekly" pokes fun at their claims to fame, and Time Inc.'s shiny new digital celebrity site, Instant.me, hopes to build on their brands.

It used to be that the only way a non-recognizable person could land in the pages of the glossy celebrity magazines was to lose 100 pounds, serve as some heartwarming testimony to good-old-fashioned American values, or be murdered. But in the early aughts, the magazines started diversifying their coverage of Hollywood's leading Jens and Bens with stories on the romantic dupes and plastic surgery nightmares of reality television. Now, as the rise of social media demolishes the leverage that celebrity tabloids once had over their most famous subjects, the gossip industry keeps defining celebrity downward. (After all, no magazine can match the reach of Taylor Swift's more than 90 million Instagram fans or Kim Kardashian West's 47 million Twitter followers.)

When Ms. Kardashian West first rose to prominence, commentators sneered that she was "famous for nothing." The accusation seems quaint now: Tabloids have moved on from covering reality television stars like Ms. Kardashian West to following reality TV supporting characters, former reality TV stars, friends and exes of former reality TV stars — even people who post their own family dramas straight to YouTube. These days, gossip sites are also fueled by figures largely famous for doing nothing much. Jeremy Meeks, whose image went viral when Twitter swooned for his hot mug shot, has popped up on the websites of Us Weekly and People since his release from prison earlier this year. Instagram models like Ms. Richie, Sahara Ray and Bronte Blampied can milk months of coverage out of a couple of shots of themselves posing with Mr. Bieber.

And Refinery29 recently ran a photo-laden spread on the "Gucci Gang," a group of four stylish 14-to-16-year-old Parisian girls whose central accomplishment is attracting a combined 50,000 Instagram followers. As the de facto crew leader, Angelina Woreth, put it, "It's easy to hate us, actually, because we are not doing something, we're not really doing anything."

Across the web, a new gossip press further enables these lesser celebrity castes. Drama generated by the young stars of YouTube, Vine and Musical.ly churns through nimble aggregation centers like Superfame and Trending All Day. The freewheeling Guru Gossip forum cuts through the glittery facade of online beauty gurus, while Get Off My Internets deflates the egos of the lifestyle-blogging set. And The Shade

Room, a social-media gossip site focusing on black celebrities, pulls in 6.1 million Instagram followers. While it posts plenty of news on known quantities (Beyoncé, Drake, Kevin Durant), it recognizes that some of the juiciest material comes from the smaller players (Tameka Harris, Karlie Redd, Keke Wyatt) who keep their names circulating on Twitter by spilling their guts on Instagram.

Then there is "Who? Weekly," the cutting podcast in which the hosts, Lindsey Weber and Bobby Finger, guide listeners through celebrity's confounding new frontier. The podcast's name derives from the typical reaction of a layperson to reading a noncelebrity's name in the news. As the hosts explained in a handy primer published in July, "the subjects of gossip coverage can be divided into two categories: Whos (as in: *furrows brow* *Who?*) and Thems (as in: 'Oh, *them*.')"

On a recent episode, they take on Brittany Farrar, the ex-girlfriend of Aaron Rodgers's little brother, Jordan Rodgers (who is now dating the "Bachelorette" star JoJo Fletcher), who recently accused Jordan of cheating in a series of Instagram posts. "Why are we still hearing about her?" Ms. Weber asked. Mr. Finger replied: "Because she wants us — she did her due diligence in making sure we talked about her." And just like that: A Who was born.

Legacy media companies are dancing as fast as they can to keep up. In May, Time Inc. debuted Instant.me, dedicated to covering the foot soldiers of social media. Instant sells its subjects — a constellation of YouTube creators, Snapchat fitness models and Instagram-famous pets — as "The New Famous." It's illustrated with a Tumblr aesthetic (dancing pizzas, glimmering diamonds, waving koalas) and littered with kissy-face emoji. The institutional voice is synergetic teen-speak, like: "We're hungryyyyyy and these slow cooker chicken tamales from Cooking Light sound amazinggggg." (Cooking Light is a Time Inc. property.) The site is sponsored exclusively by Degree, and every few minutes, Instant.me's social stars jump eagerly into a deodorant ad.

Instant's prerogative is to constantly surface social faces (the recurring segment "Who to Follow" offers dossiers on emerging talents) while inspiring Instant viewers to join their ranks ("Just the Tip," another segment, gives advice on how to build your own social fandom). A grown-up can watch Instant.me for hours without seeing a recognizable name, and that's kind of the point. "The goal with Instant is for my grandmother to be able to go onto the site and enjoy herself and get caught up," Kirstin Benson, Instant's editorial director, told Adweek in July.

Time Inc. has started a kind of general-interest publication on the internet-famous just as the internet has atomized celebrity into a zillion tiny fandoms. Few people are typically energized by the generic category of "social media figure." They get their kicks by closely following a select few of their favorite stars, the stars' friends and family, and a network of (often infighting) fans. The obsessive monitoring of all these channels drums up sufficient drama to create an enduring story line, even if only a few thousand people can manage to follow along. Plus, the setup provides fans the illusion of power in determining which Whos become Thems (Blac Chyna, a rap video vixen engaged to Rob Kardashian, is on her way toward top-level recognition) and which seem destined to fade into permanent obscurity (I'm sorry, Sarah Wright Olsen).

But these modern fandoms produce grist for non-fans, too. There's something deliciously surreal about monitoring the online movements of the barely famous, a class of people who are just unpolished, desperate and savvy enough to act mad, sloppy and sexy. The fact that publications like People and Us Weekly are covering it with a straight face adds another absurd layer.

Besides, these people are assaulting our social feeds every day whether we like it or not. Outlets like The Shade Room and "Who? Weekly" have managed to extract bits of hilarity, delight and shame out of that arid media landscape. They have intuited what the traditional tabloids don't quite get: The pursuit of celebrity has emerged as a grand tabloid narrative in and of itself.

How Cats Evolved to Win the Internet

OPINION | BY ABIGAIL TUCKER | OCT. 15, 2016

LIKE MANY PEOPLE, I needed a cat photo for my personal website. Lulu did the trick. She was puffy, orange and belonged to the ex-roommate of my sister's boyfriend. Lulu — whose nickname is Luyoncé — vamped obligingly, and Lulu's owner soon decided that her budding cat model required an Instagram account.

That was just over six months ago. My website's traffic has languished, but Lulu now commands nearly 40,000 Instagram followers. "Be the cute you wish to see in this world," one post says. In another, she gloats from the bottom of a laundry hamper.

The glorious rise of my furry affiliate came as a bit of a shock, and I'm not alone in my consternation. Nobody intended for the internet to be swarmed with cats. (Asked what surprised him most about online life, the digital pioneer Tim Berners-Lee replied, "Kittens.") Yet here they are, modeling toupees made from their own discarded fur as part of the Trump Your Cat movement or popping up to protest Brexit.

Of course nobody intended for the planet to be swarmed with house cats either. In many ways, their online dominance is an extension of their earthly conquests, and the same flesh-and-blood behavior that propelled cats across the globe also sustains Lulu and her peers.

A recent study of ancient feline DNA showed how cats left their native lands in the Near East, hitching rides with human seafarers — including, delightfully, Vikings — and then ditching us to invade an ever-wider array of habitats.

This is pretty much what happened on the internet. The online community 4Chan is thought to have introduced the LOLcat (the "laughing out loud" cat) in the mid-2000s as an inside joke. But the LOLcats escaped and spread and multiplied, just like the Viking cats or Australia's colonial-era cat castaways, which have become nearly 20 million strays today.

OLIVIER SCHRAUWEN

Cats aren't the only creatures to thrive online, of course, and dogs actually eclipse them in search traffic. But their viral success is unique. According to data from Buzzfeed, the most popular cat posts get almost quadruple the traffic of the most-clicked dogs. Cat images also have unparalleled staying power. Other creature memes — the "O Rly" snowy owl, the Socially Awkward Penguin — tend to rise and fall rather quickly. But cats remain on top, pixelated apex predators whose peaks of online attention last for months or years.

Their virtual success is rooted in their real biology. Cats are solitary, asocial hypercarnivores built to do one thing: get meat. The famous cat meme I Can Haz Cheeseburger, in which a gaping gray cat demands a quarter-pounder, had the right idea. Every fiber of the feline being is evolved to hunt, and cats employ a distinctive stalk-and-ambush approach, in which they sit very still and watch for prey to innocently wander by, then explode from the underbrush to slaughter it.

This stalking and pouncing is perfect for a six-second Vine or a pithy tweet. Think of your favorite YouTube cat videos: A cat springs into a box, or bops a baby on the head without warning, or rockets out from beneath the bed. What you're watching is an ambush.

Dogs, by contrast, aren't surprise predators. Their wild relatives, wolves, are long-distance hunters, tracking prey for miles. Such dogged personalities make for better long narrative arcs, which is why canines outnumber cats in movies and novels. But the internet is more like poetry: nonlinear, fragmented, spontaneous and explosive, a place to simultaneously hide and strike. And from Dr. Seuss to T. S. Eliot, poetry is a rare medium in which cats are more prevalent than dogs.

Cats' social habits — or rather, lack thereof — also prime them for life online. Dogs are highly social animals, whose behavior is such a mirror of our own emotions that without people in close physical proximity they can seem like unfinished beings.

Cats, though, are self-contained. Because cats need staggering quantities of meat, they are by necessity solitary, patrolling large tracts of territory alone. They perform best in perfect isolation, and we get almost the same satisfaction admiring a cat through a computer screen as we do from observing one lolling on our own carpet.

But what about the quintessential internet artifact, cat photos? These portraits involve neither socializing nor violence. Yet their appeal is still connected to feline biology, through the mesmerizing structure of the feline face.

As watch-and-wait hunters, cats have big, round eyes planted right in the center of their heads, giving them excellent depth perception when they leap for a kill. They have little snub noses, since they lurk in hiding places instead of snuffling after prey for miles like dogs. And they have rounded faces and chubby "cheeks," the byproduct of short, powerful jaws designed to deliver a killing bite.

These facial features, a terrifying distillation of feline lethality, happen to also be what humans consider cute. They remind us of own faces, and especially of our babies, since humans, too, have big eyes planted in the center of our heads, which we use in large part to read the facial expressions of others. Through this uncanny but accidental interspecies resemblance, cat faces prime us to communicate, whether by post, tweet or pin.

In nature cats themselves aren't big communicators. Most interact with other members of their own species only when they fight or mate. Unlike group-living dogs, which have a large, expressive repertoire, cats have faces that are empty canvases, as the animal behaviorist John Bradshaw suggests — strikingly human but also perpetually deadpan.

This is why cat photos seem to cry out for captioning: We feel moved to fill in their blanks.

Hello Kitty, whose popularity anticipated the success of online cats, exaggerates this beguiling blankness by having no mouth at all. But we are also transfixed by cats whose captions seem built in. Many A-list internet felines, like Grumpy Cat, have oral deformities that make them seem to smile or grimace, as if they're furry emoticons.

Though cats were predestined for online dominance, they might have missed the boat had the internet started a little earlier. Until the last half-century or so, most pet cats lived outdoors, and — precisely because cats are cryptic loners, and largely nocturnal to boot — we seldom saw them for extended periods. Only recently, with the advent of the "indoor cat," have we finally gained round-the-clock access, and the ability to immortalize our cornered pets' every move.

But as ever with the cat, these photos and cellphone movies give us only the illusion of control. Stranded in our living rooms but loosed online, cats slip our grasp yet again.

ABIGAIL TUCKER is the author of the book "The Lion in the Living Room: How House Cats Tamed Us and Took Over the World," from which this essay is adapted.

The Rise and (Maybe) Fall of Influencers

BY VANESSA FRIEDMAN | MAY 10, 2017

I NEVER REALLY expected to write these words, but: It was Kendall Jenner who did it for me.

Or, to be fair, not Kendall Jenner herself — or not entirely Kendall Jenner — but rather the 10th-anniversary Indian Vogue cover that featured Kendall Jenner, as conceived and photographed by Mario Testino. When released last week on the magazine's social media accounts, it almost immediately became the center of a storm of social media ire, most of it along the lines of this tweet: "Disgustingly inappropriate. Were ALL the Indian women unavailable??"

Which was then followed, as these things so often are, by a host of headlines like CNN.com's "Vogue India Cover Lands Kendall Jenner in More Trouble."

But here's the thing: Was it really Ms. Jenner's fault? Was she in any way culpable for this bad choice? After all, she was being used as work for hire: a body and a face to sell a magazine.

Or was she?

Therein lies the problem. Because the obvious assumption — the one made by all the worked-up folks in the Twittersphere — was that she had been employed not just as a clothes hanger (as models used to be known), but, at least in part, as herself: a public figure with an immediately recognizable name and face and family back story, along with approximately 80.3 million Instagram followers. An — and I cringe at the word, but it is in the Cambridge English Dictionary — Influencer. And that influence was part of what Indian Vogue was paying for by paying her to be on its cover.

It's the same thing that the Fyre Festival, the famously failed music festival in the Bahamas, was paying for when it paid Ms. Jenner, along with Bella Hadid (12.7 million Instagram followers), Hailey Baldwin

(10 million) and Emily Ratajkowski (12.8 million), to drum up excitement via promotional posts with said women cavorting in bikinis on a beach. It's what, to a certain extent, Pepsi was paying for when it hired Ms. Jenner (sense a theme here?) and put her in an ill-conceived ad in which she uses a soda to soften up a police officer at a protest. It's what Vogue Arabia was paying for when it put an only-semi-veiled Gigi Hadid on the cover of its first issue.

Whether it is obviously an ad, whether a Federal Trade Commission-required hashtag admission goes with it or not (and the F.T.C. is increasingly cracking down on influencer posts, recently writing to 45 celebrities to warn them about necessary disclosures), there is, as Lucie Greene, the worldwide director of the Innovation Group at J. Walter Thompson, said, "an implied individual choice."

And that means that those involved are perceived as having a personal — not merely professional — relationship with the thing they are selling. Which in turn means they bear some responsibility for it. There is a downside to the upside of being an influencer.

Sometimes it's literal: The Fyre Festival is now facing a class-action lawsuit in which the defendants include not only the organizers, but also a number of "Jane Does" who helped promote the festival.

Sometimes it's reputational: After Selena Gomez, the proud possessor of the most Instagram followers badge (she had 120 million as of Wednesday), signed on to represent Coach — after having been an ambassador for Louis Vuitton, a brand with a very different aesthetic, one nonfan tweeted: "Selena Gomez, the previous face of Coca Cola, Louis Vuitton, Verizon, and the current face of Pantene and Coach ... a joke to the industry???"

Either way, it's real. As with all slippery slopes, it's easy to hop on but also easy to end up in a heap at the bottom. Which raises the possibility that we are on the verge of a new (hopefully more considered) age in the evolution of Influencer culture.

"The influencer bubble will totally collapse in the next 12 months if people aren't very careful about the money being thrown around as

BENJAMIN NORMAN FOR THE NEW YORK TIMES

Selena Gomez, with the Weeknd at the Met Gala this month, has been criticized for being the face of too many brands.

brands try to buy influencer placement," said Caroline Issa, the fashion director and chief executive of Tank magazine and a street-style star-turned-occasional Influencer.

Since being what used to be called a "tastemaker" became a job, and word-of-mouth tips became known as "influencer marketing," attention has been focused largely on the risks to brands in linking up with individuals. See, for example, the lesson of PewDiePie, a YouTube star who had signed deals with Disney and Google and then was discovered to have made anti-Semitic statements. (The corporate brands cut all ties, not surprisingly.)

But while it's easy to be distracted by the siren call of Influencer culture — Money for just being you! Free trips to sit front row at fashion shows! Global branding laying out the red carpet for your delicately pointed feet! — what the cases of Kendall et al. make clear is that there are also risks to individuals.

As Meridith Valiando Rojas, the co-founder and chief executive of DigiTour Media, the live entertainment company that runs Digifest, the Coachella of the YouTube generation, said, being an Influencer means you are often thought of as a "friend" by your followers. And that comes with a host of expectations that may not attach to a more traditional kind of talent.

"Youth culture can see through anything they think is inauthentic," Ms. Greene said. And because followers have what at least seems to be direct access to their "friend" on Twitter or Instagram, they can respond directly. Also publicly.

As we go further down the rabbit hole of personal branding, new agencies are springing up with the mission of connecting brands to influencers and monetizing social media presence (names like Muse-Find, UP Influence and Instabrand), and traditional talent agencies like CAA and WME/IMG are signing up YouTube stars or helping their clients transform themselves into social media mavens. Magazines and ad agencies are measuring a model's attraction not just by his or her physical dimensions, but also by the number of followers. It is increasingly clear that a disconnect exists between the imperative to make as much money as possible out of your influence as fast as possible, and the need to be highly selective about how you wield your influence in order to preserve its equity.

The generation that grew up on social media, the digital natives at whom Digifest is aimed, understands this viscerally. The older generation, the ones who Ms. Rojas said "were born not on social platforms but as traditional celebrities, and have migrated to social afterward," seems to be learning the hard way. And that may, in the end, change the equation. Or at least … well, influence it.

Sorry. Couldn't resist.

Inside the Hollywood Home of Social Media's Stars. (Don't Be Shy.)

BY DAISUKE WAKABAYASHI | DEC. 30, 2017

LOS ANGELES — On any given day, something crazy is likely to be happening at 1600 Vine Street, a 550-unit apartment complex in Hollywood.

A scary-looking clown might be shimmying across a narrow ledge eight floors above the sidewalk, or a young woman dangling from a balcony while a masked man wields a knife. A husky dog with pink ears, a pony, a baby monkey and other exotic animals also call it home.

But you don't need to live there to experience the high jinks, because they are available for anyone to watch on YouTube, Instagram and whatever social media platform comes next. The building at 1600 Vine functions as dormitory and studio lot for some of the internet's biggest stars.

Videos shot there have been watched billions of times. The common spaces — a spacious gym, walkways lined with beige blocks and a courtyard surrounded by lush plants — are so recognizable that it's like walking onto the set of a popular TV show.

The list of current and former residents is a who's who of social media celebrities: the brothers Logan Paul and Jake Paul, Amanda Cerny, Juanpa Zurita, Lele Pons and Andrew Bachelor, known as King Bach.

Some are comedians, some are models, and some are famous for being famous. But all are so-called influencers, social media speak for people with a huge digital audience.

1600 Vine offers a peek into the booming ecosystem of these social media stars. As in any caldron of attention seekers who live and work together in the same building, it's an atmosphere rife with cliquishness, jealousy, insecurity and the social hierarchy of high school, except everyone knows precisely how popular (or unpopular) you are. And it's amplified by the fact that influencers can become millionaires with a following on a par with any movie star's.

PETER HORVATH

Joshua Cohen, a founder of Tubefilter, a site that tracks the online video industry, described the talent at 1600 Vine as a modern-day version of the Brat Pack or the Mickey Mouse Club.

"You have all these people in the same environment who grew up together and getting their entertainment chops together," Mr. Cohen said. "Now, they're some of the biggest people on whatever platform they're on."

GAINING FOLLOWERS

The origins of 1600 Vine as a social media launching pad are rooted, appropriately enough, in the video platform Vine.

Around 2014, the stars of Vine's six-second videos started flocking to Los Angeles to turn a hobby into a career. A few of the early stars moved into this contemporary, amenity-rich complex, above a Trader Joe's and between Jimmy Durante and Clark Gable on the Hollywood Walk of Fame.

Within a few months, the apartments — notable for their floor-to-

MOLLY MATALON FOR THE NEW YORK TIMES

Katie, left, and Bri Teresi, sisters and swimsuit models who live at 1600 Vine, were tapped by a neighbor to appear in an Instagram video that has been viewed more than two million times.

ceiling windows, modern kitchens and living spaces, and common areas that include a pool and hot tub — became a recognizable backdrop to the most popular Vine videos. It wasn't long before 1600 Vine became the place to be.

It remained that way even after Vine shut down in 2016.

One of the early stars was Ms. Cerny, 26, who moved to Los Angeles from Florida four years ago to become an actress. Rejected by agents for a lack of experience, the former model started making Vine videos. Her goofy comedy sketches were a hit, and she moved into 1600 Vine to be closer to other Vine stars.

"It was perfect — we could film wherever, whenever," she said. "Being able to surround yourself with other creative people helps."

These days, Ms. Cerny is in the top tier of influencers, with 18.8 million Instagram followers and 1.1 million subscribers to her YouTube vlogs, the popular YouTube format that marries a daily diary with the artificial drama of reality TV. Sponsors like Guess jeans pay her six figures for promoting their products.

Hanging out at 1600 Vine can open doors, too. A year ago, the actor Ray Diaz had only 5,000 followers on Instagram, even though he was a regular on "East Los High," a show on Hulu. Then one day, while he was lifting weights in the building's gym (a friend of his lived there), he met Ms. Pons, a 21-year-old YouTube comedian with 20.9 million Instagram followers. Ms. Pons invited him to appear in her video "My Big Fat Hispanic Family," a skit about introducing a boyfriend to her eccentric family and friends.

The video has had more than 12 million views, and soon Mr. Diaz became an influencer on his own, reaching more than one million Instagram followers a few months after it was posted. Still, Mr. Diaz wanted more, even after landing a regular role on "Lopez," a comedy on TV Land. So last December, he moved to 1600 Vine, to one of the nicer, split-level two-bedroom units on the 10th floor.

Today, he has 3.2 million followers and boasts that he went from driving for Uber to driving a Bentley. "Instagram is what pays for the penthouse," he added.

Success stories like Mr. Diaz's are the reason wannabe influencers continue flocking to 1600 Vine, paying anywhere from $2,500 to $15,000 a month. Many aspiring photographers and video editors hang out in the common areas, hoping to get a foot in the door by working with a few prominent influencers.

The complex is one of many modern apartment buildings in the Hollywood area. There is always the whisper that some other, nearby building is the new hot spot with more welcoming rules for social media stars, but 1600 Vine remains the most prominent and best known.

In June, Bri and Katie Teresi, sisters and swimsuit models, moved into a small one-bedroom apartment, paying $2,700 a month, after they got a taste of what being around other influencers could do for them. Josh Paler Lin, a friend in the building, tapped them to appear in a video in which a Lamborghini's exhaust blows off their clothes. It garnered more than two million views, and the sisters said they had each added 10,000 followers.

"Right now, I'm focused on growing and really getting my numbers up," said Bri Teresi, 23, who has 419,000 followers on Instagram.

Others see living at 1600 Vine as a golden marketing opportunity.

Taylor Offer and Parker Burr moved in last year hoping to befriend social media stars not for their own fame but to promote their sock company, Feat Socks. When Mr. Offer first visited the two-bedroom unit, he said, it was like "walking into Jerry's apartment building on 'Seinfeld' " because he recognized it from Vine videos. He signed a lease on the spot, needing to prove only that he and Mr. Burr could afford the $3,700 monthly rent.

But Mr. Offer soon realized it wasn't enough to live in the building; they had to help the influencers fill their daily need for content. So Mr. Offer bought a cute English bulldog puppy and a flashy Polaris Slingshot car. The puppy appeared in a video with Ms. Cerny while Logan Paul took an interest in the purple car, a three-wheeled vehicle that looks like a roadster.

A star like Mr. Paul has his pick of sponsorship deals, but he took a liking to his new neighbors, so he concocted a bet — or, more accurately, a social media story line. If Mr. Paul could sell 20,000 pairs of socks (printed with an image of his colorful parrot, Maverick), he would get the roadster. He promoted the bet in videos and, even though he fell short, Feat had its best sales month ever and Mr. Paul received a $200,000 commission check.

"As a business expense," Mr. Offer said, "this place pays for itself."

REALITY SHOW

Calling 1600 Vine home is still no guarantee of influencer status. It also breeds a certain kind of cliquishness and backbiting.

Gregg Martin, a young actor who has landed bit roles in TV series including "Agents of S.H.I.E.L.D.," said he felt the building's stars looked down on him. He has 44,000 Instagram followers.

“That’s considered laughable for most people here,” he said. “People kind of look at you and just see the numbers.”

One influencer told him that he was following too many people on Instagram. It made him seem desperate. “I thought he was joking,” he said. “But he was dead serious.”

The building also attracts its share of fame seekers, like the Justin Bieber impersonator who has all the same tattoos as the actual singer and is often seen visiting a friend in the building.

It is also a magnet for bizarre behavior that doesn’t exactly make for good neighbors. Social media stars need daily content lest they be forgotten. It’s a dynamic that pushes them to do increasingly outrageous things to capture attention.

Consider Logan Paul, one of YouTube’s biggest stars, with close to 15 million subscribers to his channel. His escalating stunts in March alone included dangling a $20 bill from his balcony using a fishing rod to tempt passers-by, rigging a zip line over Hollywood Boulevard to send gifts to fans camped outside and pretending to be shot as fans watched in horror outside his window.

Building management told Mr. Paul that it was not renewing his lease. Naturally, he recorded the conversation for his vlog, before he moved to the building next door. (He was asked to leave there, too.)

After other neighbors started to complain, management has also limited where residents can shoot. First, it banned filming by the courtyard pool. Then it banned large professional cameras in all common areas. And in June, management went further and now requires residents to seek permission before shooting any video in common areas.

Danielle Guttman Klein, chairwoman of Klein Financial Corporation, which oversees the property’s management, said it needed to walk a fine line between embracing its stars and protecting the interests of tenants whose day jobs don’t revolve around getting likes on Facebook.

The influencers seem to sympathize, at least for now. Ms. Cerny said that she had been threatened with eviction but that management had allowed her to stay when she promised to not film in any of the common areas. But she said she could understand why many of the big stars had moved out.

"It does get overwhelming sometimes," she said. "Eventually, you need somewhere to go and not post about your life for a second."

Logan Paul, YouTube Star, Says Posting Video of Dead Body Was 'Misguided'

BY JONAH ENGEL BROMWICH | JAN. 2, 2018

A YOUTUBE STAR with millions of followers apologized on Monday for posting a video that showed a dead body hanging from a tree in a Japanese forest known as a destination for suicide victims.

Logan Paul, 22, posted an apology on Twitter after the video attracted a torrent of criticism online, saying that he had published it in an attempt to raise awareness about suicide and suicide prevention.

"I was misguided by shock and awe, as portrayed in the video," he said. "I still am."

In another video, posted on Tuesday, Mr. Paul again apologized, this time specifically to the dead man and his family. He also asked his fans to stop defending him.

"I should have never posted the video. I should have put the cameras down," he said.

The original video, which has since been removed from YouTube but is available elsewhere online, begins with Mr. Paul warning viewers that the following footage is graphic.

"This definitely marks a moment in YouTube history," he says. "Because I'm pretty sure that this has never hopefully happened to anyone on YouTube ever."

"Now with that said, buckle up," Mr. Paul adds, cursing for effect.

As the video proceeds, Mr. Paul describes the reputation of the Aokigahara forest, which has become well-known in the past decade as a destination for people looking to kill themselves.

In 2016 alone, three North American films were set in the forest, which lies at the base of Mount Fuji, a sacred site in Japan.

Local folk tales have also fueled talk about the paranormal within the forest, a subject that Mr. Paul eagerly latches onto as he and his companions begin their trek with a guide.

In the next scene, they come across the body. The face is blurred; the rest is left visible. Mr. Paul and the others react in shock and Mr. Paul urges the guide to call the police.

"Yo, are you alive?" he shouts toward the body.

As a camera pans over the body, which Mr. Paul later says is only about 100 yards away from the parking lot, he describes its condition, and speculates that the death was recent. He apologizes to his viewers and says that suicide, depression and mental illness are not a joke.

As the group leaves the area where the body was found, Mr. Paul, who has television experience and has trained with comedy troupes, begins to engage in the kinds of behavior most familiar to his viewers: exaggerated reaction shots and nervous laughter. The tone soon becomes more antic as Mr. Paul and the others appear to try to lighten the mood.

Toward the end of the video, Mr. Paul says that his smiling and laughing "is not a portrayal of how I feel about the circumstances," describing it as his coping mechanism.

The video, which was posted on Sunday, quickly received pushback online, as people reacted to Mr. Paul's decision to show the body and his capering afterward. Some shared numbers for suicide hotlines and told stories about their own struggles with mental illness.

YouTube said in a statement that the video had violated its policies, which prohibit "violent or gory content posted in a shocking, sensational or disrespectful manner."

"Our hearts go out to the family of the person featured in the video," the statement said.

Mr. Paul's YouTube channel has more than 15 million subscribers, making him even more popular than his younger brother, Jake, who may be more well-known to those who do not regularly watch vlogs thanks to his own brushes with controversy.

YouTube stars are often incentivized to post increasingly eye-catching footage in a bid for subscribers, who are attracted to more outlandish clips. After Jake Paul drew the attention of mainstream news outlets over the summer for, essentially, annoying his neighbors on camera, he posted another video in which he tried to convince people that he had been arrested, upping the ante after the surge of press.

The brothers' audiences are largely made up of younger people. Toward the end of the Japan video, Logan Paul runs into a young fan in the parking lot who is with an older chaperone.

"I have one piece of advice," he tells them, smiling and pointing to where the body is. "Don't go over there."

Don’t Scoff at Influencers. They’re Taking Over the World.

COLUMN | BY KEVIN ROOSE | JULY 16, 2019

As social media expands its cultural dominance, the people who can steer the online conversation will have an upper hand.

ANAHEIM, CALIF. — When the first TikTok star is elected president, I hope she will save some room in her cabinet for older and more conventional bureaucrats, even if they don’t have millions of followers, great hair or amazing dance moves.

I say “when,” not “if,” because I just spent three days at VidCon, the annual social media convention in Anaheim, hanging out with a few thousand current and future internet celebrities. And it’s increasingly obvious to me that the teenagers and 20-somethings who have mastered these platforms — and who are often dismissed as shallow, preening narcissists by adults who don’t know any better — are going to dominate not just internet culture or the entertainment industry but society as a whole.

On the surface, this can be a terrifying proposition. One day at VidCon, I hung out with a crew of teenage Instagram stars, who seemed to spend most of their time filming “collabs” with other creators and complimenting one another on their “drip,” influencer-speak for clothes and accessories. (In their case, head-to-toe Gucci and Balenciaga outfits with diamond necklaces and designer sneakers.) Another day, I witnessed an awkward dance battle between two budding TikTok influencers, neither of whom could have been older than 10. (Adults who are just catching up: TikTok is a short-form video app owned by the Chinese internet company Bytedance.)

But if you can look past the silliness and status-seeking, many people at VidCon are hard at work. Being an influencer can be an exhausting, burnout-inducing job, and the people who are good at it have typically spent years working their way up the ladder. Many social media influencers are essentially one-person start-ups, and the best ones can spot trends, experiment relentlessly with new formats and platforms, build an authentic connection with an audience, pay close attention to their channel analytics, and figure out how to distinguish themselves in a crowded media environment — all while churning out a constant stream of new content.

Not all influencers are brilliant polymaths, of course. Some of them have succeeded by virtue of being conventionally attractive, or good at video games, or in possession of some other surface-level attribute. Others have made their names with dubious stunts and extreme political commentary.

But as social media expands its cultural dominance, the people who can steer the online conversation will have an upper hand in whatever niche they occupy — whether that's media, politics, business or some other field.

"The way to think of influencers or creators is as entrepreneurs," said Chris Stokel-Walker, the author of "YouTubers." "These people are setting up businesses, hiring staff, managing budgets. These are massively transferable skills."

Just look at Representative Alexandria Ocasio-Cortez, the New York Democrat who has become a powerful force in Congress by pairing her policy agenda with an intuitive understanding of what works online. Or look at what's happening in Brazil, where YouTubers are winning political elections by mobilizing their online fan bases.

In the business world, influencer culture is already an established force. A generation of direct-to-consumer brands that were built using the tools and tactics of social media has skyrocketed to success — like Glossier, the influencer-beloved beauty company that recently raised $100 million at a valuation of more than $1 billion, or Away, the luggage start-up whose ubiquitous Instagram ads helped it reach a valuation of $1.4 billion. Many social media stars strike endorsement deals with major brands, in addition to earning money through advertising and merchandise sales. And even executives in sleepy, old-line industries now hire "personal branding consultants" to help increase their online followings.

Natalie Alzate, a YouTuber with more than 10 million subscribers who goes by Natalies Outlet, is an example of the wave of influencers who treated their online brand-building as a business rather than a fun hobby. Four years ago, when Ms. Alzate first came to VidCon, she was a marketing student with fewer than 7,000 subscribers. She decided to study her favorite YouTubers, watch how they made their videos and then test videos in multiple genres, seeing which ones performed best on her channel.

"I grew up watching people, like Michelle Phan, that were building legacies out of, honestly, just being really relatable online," Ms. Alzate said. "It was always an aspiration."

Eventually, she hit on formats — like beauty tips and lifehacks — that reliably performed well, and she was off to the races. Today, she is a full-time YouTuber with a small staff, a production studio and the kind of fame she once coveted.

In truth, influencers have been running the world for years. We just haven't called them that. Instead, we called them "movie stars" or "talk-radio hosts" or "Davos attendees." The ability to stay relevant and attract attention to your work has always been critical. And who, aside from perhaps President Trump, is better at getting attention than a YouTube star?

VidCon, which started 10 years ago as a meet-and-greet event for popular YouTubers, is a perfect place to observe influencers in their natural habitat. And many of them were here to promote their channels, to network with other creators and to make strides toward the dream of internet fame.

Sometimes, that meant appearing in photos and videos with more popular influencers in an attempt to increase their own following, a practice known in influencer circles as "clout chasing." Other times, it meant going to panels with titles like "Curating Your Personal Brand"

and “How to Go Viral and Build an Audience.” For VidCon’s featured creators, the super-famous ones with millions of followers, it can mean spending the day at a meet-and-greet with fans before going out to V.I.P. parties at night.

Not all of the young people I met at VidCon will spend their whole lives pursuing internet fame. Some of them will grow up, go off to college and wind up becoming doctors, lawyers or accountants. Some will fizzle out and be replaced by a younger generation of internet stars.

But the lessons they learned from performing on YouTube, Instagram and TikTok will stick with them, regardless of where they end up. Just as the 20th century groomed a generation of children steeped in the ethos of TV culture, the 21st century will produce a generation of business moguls, politicians and media figures who grew up chasing clout online and understand how to operate the levers of the attention economy.

“In the early days, it felt like this was a sub-niche of youth culture,” Beau Bryant, the general manager of talent at Fullscreen, a management agency for digital creators, told me at VidCon. He gestured around at a room filled with influencers sitting on velvet couches. Some were taking selfies and editing their Instagram stories. Others were holding business meetings about partnerships and sponsored content deals.

“Now, it just feels like this is what youth culture is,” Mr. Bryant said.

In other words, influencers are the future. Dismiss them at your peril.

KEVIN ROOSE is a columnist for Business Day and a writer-at-large for The New York Times Magazine. His column, “The Shift,” examines the intersection of technology, business, and culture.

CHAPTER 3

The Biggest Apps and Sites

A dizzying array of websites and apps debut on a daily basis, but only a select few of those attract the most viewers, including YouTube, Snapchat and Instagram. Popularity of these platforms among everyday watchers translates into the rise of certain celebrities. But how is such popularity judged? Numbers of followers is one way. "Klout" was another: The now-defunct website and mobile app used high-tech analytics to measure the influence and importance of these Internet personalities.

Coming Soon: Celebrity Web Networks From the Media Company Whalerock

BY BROOKS BARNES | FEB. 18, 2015

SANTA MONICA, CALIF. — An under-the-radar media company here called Whalerock could become a threat to the entertainment establishment.

Following the cut-out-the-middleman model pioneered by Glenn Beck, who left Fox News in 2011 to start his own subscription-based Internet television channel, Whalerock Industries has made deals to create similar personal networks for some big names: the Kardashian sisters, Howard Stern and the rap star Tyler, the Creator.

These channels, set to arrive in the coming months and available via the web and mobile app, will offer a mix of paid and free programming, said Lloyd Braun, the owner of Whalerock and a former senior executive at ABC and Yahoo. Depending on the channel, offerings will eventually include music, video, exclusive photos, interviews, merchandise, games and other "premium" content, Mr. Braun said.

Whalerock's longer-term goal is to shift the power — and the lion's share of the profit — away from traditional media companies and toward talent. Mr. Beck has an estimated 400,000 subscribers paying $9.95 a month for TheBlaze TV, his streaming network, and continues to host his traditional radio show. Whalerock is now trying to burst through the door he cracked open. Mr. Braun made it clear that the goal is for "the ultimate control" to lie with artists, not media companies.

He said that these "media hubs" should not antagonize the likes of NBCUniversal's E! network (home to "Keeping Up With the Kardashians"), Sirius XM Radio (Mr. Stern's home since 2006) and Sony Music Entertainment (Tyler, the Creator's label). "We are well aware that current business deals exist, and we respect them," Mr. Braun said.

The Kardashians, for instance, will continue to make their cable show, and Mr. Stern may renew his expiring contract with Sirius. "Done right, we are going to show how premium artists who want to control their media life and engage directly with their audiences can work synergistically with traditional media, resulting in a better business for everybody," Mr. Braun said this month.

Still, this is unproved territory. Among the many things that could go wrong: Fans could quickly tire of endless à la carte payments, which have a way of adding up in a hurry. Mr. Braun's plans require a real dedication over the long term from the celebrity participants. And some analysts point out that demand may be much less than anticipated; millions of followers on Twitter do not guarantee millions or even thousands of subscribers.

But Richard Greenfield, a media analyst at BTIG Research, said that Whalerock's business was threatening to traditional programmers. "For the artists who have the chutzpah to break free of the traditional models, there is a huge opportunity," he said, especially while there are still relatively few direct-to-consumer channels being offered.

Mr. Braun said he planned to create app-based channels for 12 to 20 performers and brands by 2018. If he succeeds, Whalerock could bundle the channels together in various configurations and make distribution deals with cable providers and services like Apple TV, just as Viacom and Time Warner do today with networks like MTV and CNN.

Reaching the masses used to require access to distribution. If you wanted to publish a popular book, you needed a Random House. If you wanted to release a hit song, you needed a record label. But mobile apps and the web are making distribution ubiquitous, as Netflix has proved, and Mr. Braun and others — WWE, CBS and the comedian Louis C. K. among them — are now trying to capitalize on that shift.

In particular, Whalerock is focused on a new generation of "cord nevers," people who have never paid for a standard cable TV package, and "cord cutters," who have canceled their cable service. Instead, these consumers pay only for the networks or programs they want to watch. And they decide how, when and where to watch them. Increasingly, according to Nielsen, a mobile device is the preferred viewing platform.

"I would rather be a guinea pig than spend my career rearranging the chairs on the Titanic," said Christian Clancy, a music manager whose clients include Tyler Okonma, a.k.a. Tyler, the Creator. "The problem for artists like Tyler is that once they get done paying all of these middlemen, they're not left with much."

There still is a middleman, of course: Mr. Braun, whose company will handle things like ad sales, design, marketing, e-commerce, technology infrastructure and video production. Whalerock will make money by taking a cut of the net revenue. Mr. Braun declined to be more specific; terms vary depending on the client.

For the record, Mr. Braun, a Hollywood character if there ever was one, often speaking in a near shout and gesticulating wildly, does not see himself as a middleman.

"We're not a middle," he said. "We're a facilitator." (Fun fact: Mr. Braun was the inspiration for a recurring character, Lloyd Braun, on "Seinfeld.")

To help finance Whalerock's digital expansion, Mr. Braun sold a minority stake in the company to GF Capital, a New York private equity firm that describes itself as making investments of $15 million to $50 million. It has also backed Blue Man Group and the Collective, a talent management and digital video production company.

Mr. Okonma's app will roll out by June, according to Jeff Berman, Whalerock's president. Channels for each Kardashian sister — Kim, Khloe, Kourtney, Kendall and Kylie — and Mr. Stern will follow in the months afterward.

"Each will look really, really specific," said Raphy Fedida, Whalerock's head of design.

Pricing decisions are still being made. Nearly all of the channels will be supported by advertising and free to consumers. Many will also sell subscriptions for premium offerings and special offers, like a pay-per-view concert or exclusive merchandise.

Programming is similarly a work in progress. But Kim Kardashian West's hub, for instance, is expected to offer photos, video and, perhaps, city guides — where she ate, where she slept — and makeup tutorials.

"I see what we do on social media as the appetizer," said Khloe Kardashian. "This is the whole dinner. Not everything we do can be captured in an Instagram shot." Added Kim Kardashian West: "This isn't about doing another website. It's about creating a digital destination."

(Skeptics who wonder whether there will be continued demand for Ms. Kardashian West, who is anything but underexposed, might consider the surprise popularity of her smartphone game, Kim Kardashian: Hollywood. It generated $74.3 million in 2014, ranking it as one the biggest mobile gaming hits of the year, according to its maker, Glu Mobile.)

As for Mr. Stern's hub, Don Buchwald, Mr. Stern's longtime agent, in an email called Mr. Braun an executive "with great creative insight to the trends of the entertainment industry" but otherwise declined to comment on the Whalerock endeavor.

Founded in 2007 as BermanBraun — Mr. Braun bought out his original partner, Gail Berman, in early 2014 — Whalerock has about 170 employees. The company is best known for creating a portfolio of websites like Wonderwall, focused on celebrity news, and Purple Clover, a site aimed at people over the age of 50.

Whalerock also has a television and movie division. Projects include "BattleBots," a robot reality show for ABC, and an espionage thriller in partnership with Metro-Goldwyn-Mayer called "I Am Pilgrim." Mr. Braun is also a producer of "Fish in the Dark," Larry David's new Broadway comedy.

Given its dual focus on technology and traditional entertainment, Whalerock may be uniquely positioned to pursue direct-to-consumer channels.

"Most of the traditional media companies are in the business of protecting the status quo," Mr. Clancy said. "That's definitely not Whalerock."

The Best Apps for Delivering Celebrity News

COLUMN | BY KIT EATON | FEB. 24, 2016

EVERYONE LOVES A BIT of celebrity-watching, and the Oscars give us plenty of excuses to do so. One great way to keep on top of all the gossip is through an app, and there are plenty of them out there catering to our curiosity about the Academy Awards and the entertainment industry.

Among all the apps promising to deliver celebrity news, the **WhoSay** app stands out for one interesting reason: Its material is supplied by the celebrities themselves. The makers of WhoSay promise that more than 1,600 well-known names use the app to share photos, videos and news with their fans.

The app's home page is an image-heavy, scrollable feed that contains updates from its famous users, along with other content like galleries and Q. and A. sessions. You can scroll through collected news on the home page, view only trending stories, explore the app's content by categories like "film" and "rising stars" or just search for news on a particular celebrity.

Tapping on an article lets you read it in more detail, and see more photos or videos.

In some ways, WhoSay is like a regular news app that's celebrity-centric, but it has celebrity input, and feels very lighthearted and fun. Unlike other apps in this category, it doesn't take itself too seriously, or go over the top with celebrity obsessions. And while there are already Oscar-related articles in the app, it is also great for keeping up with news on fashion models, sports stars and other famous people. It is free on both iOS and Android.

FirstLook Celebrity Photos and Videos is another useful celebrity news app. With its many sources and up-to-the-minute updates, the app is supposed to give you the feeling that you're among the first to see relevant articles, photos and videos from big events like the Oscars.

Because of its clean interface — with emphasis on plenty of white space and photos — this app feels more like a digital magazine than a website, and its scrolling design makes it easy to scan through the news and spot interesting items.

The app has a clever way to connect you to news about particular celebrities. A photo containing Ariana Grande and Tony Bennett, for example, is accompanied by a button that lets you follow each celebrity in your news feed, to get future content.

Clicking on the app's "Explore" tab is the trick for seeing event-specific news. Right now this shows lots of Grammy information and photos from New York Fashion Week. Soon, this is where you'll find many Oscar-related items. FirstLook also has a social media component, where you can collect "followers" of your own who want to see what you have "favorited" in the news feeds.

FirstLook is fun to use, though scrolling through the news pages can be a bit slow. Videos play automatically, which can make surprisingly loud soundtracks burst from your phone's speakers. FirstLook is free on iOS, but it isn't available on Android.

For a more traditional celebrity news app, check out **E! Online**, which is free for iOS and Android devices. It has been popular for a while, and its design reflects the same professional look and feel that E!'s TV channel has.

The app has content covering general entertainment news, photos from events and live feeds that are useful when it is awards time.

The app is free, but this means it sometimes feels like a big advertisement for associated E! shows. The news articles are written in a style that has all the hallmarks of typical celebrity news coverage, including an overdose of exclamation points. Of course E! does live event coverage rather well, so if you can deal with the few downsides to this app, like slow load times, it is worth trying out for Oscars night.

Finally, the venerable Internet Movie Database has a fabulous app that will be invaluable during the Oscars.

IMDb Movies and TV has the same detailed movie information as the famous IMDb website, so you can amuse yourself by browsing through movie trivia or details about an actor's life during the boring bits of the awards show.

The IMDb app also has a good news service as part of its home page. This offers articles from different online sources in one convenient list. The articles tend to be more serious and readable than other entertainment apps. The articles are also clearly attributed, so it is easy to go to the source website to read longer articles.

You can filter the app's feed to see trending news, movie news and news about celebrities in general or to search for your particular interests. IMDb is fast, fascinating and easy to use. It is free on iOS and Android. And if you want to see any of the Oscar-winning films, the app can help with that, too.

QUICK CALL

Animated GIF keyboards for iOS are two a penny, but the **Walkie** app is set apart by its pedigree: Its cute, dancing emoji characters are animated by former Pixar staff members. The emoji are delightful, and stand apart from rival GIFs. It is free on iOS.

Snapchat Plays Hard to Get With Celebrities and Influencers

BY KATIE BENNER AND SAPNA MAHESHWARI | DEC. 18, 2016

SAN FRANCISCO — The musician Jay Sean has visited the headquarters of YouTube, Facebook and Twitter. Instagram has reached out to tutor him on the best time to post photos for maximum impact.

But there is one social media service Mr. Sean has not heard from, even though he frequently uses the app to post spontaneous snippets of his life: Snapchat.

"When it comes to celebrities, Snapchat is different from Instagram or Twitter," said Mr. Sean, whose biggest hit was the song "Down," which also features the hip-hop artist Lil Wayne. Mr. Sean has 472,000 followers on Instagram, but he says he does not know how many people follow him on Snapchat because the company does not disclose the information.

Social networks have traditionally formed tight bonds with actors, musicians, politicians and people who are known for nothing besides their online presence, because these people have the power to draw in more users. But Snapchat, whose parent company Snap is headed toward a blockbuster initial public offering next year, is bending those rules.

Instead of giving celebrities like Mr. Sean special treatment, Snapchat limits their perks and treats them like typical users. Instead of courting influencers, who are regular people with large followings on social media and who often promote products, the app is taking a hands-off approach with them.

The reason for the difference: Snapchat wants to provide a more authentic experience, one that does not depend on whether a celebrity is on its service, and one that is not cluttered by adlike endorsements from influencers. The more someone's real life shows up on its service, Snapchat figures, the more intimate and personal it feels. And marketers may be more attracted to this authenticity, spurring them to buy

BRYAN ANSELM FOR THE NEW YORK TIMES

Jay Sean, a musician, was courted by social networks like Facebook, but Snapchat has kept its distance.

ads from Snapchat rather than pay celebrities and influencers to do product placements.

"Snapchat serves a different purpose," Mr. Sean said. "On Snapchat, I really know my fans. They don't like anything too contrived or too staged on Snapchat."

Snapchat says it prefers that celebrities use the app like everyday users, rather than as a platform to sell products. The company's terms of service prohibit getting paid to post, making influencer marketing a no-no. The company, based in Venice, Calif., said it does not want to harm Snapchat's image as a place where people go to interact with their friends.

"Snapchat is now in a very big battle for habitual users," said Grant Owens, the chief strategy officer of Critical Mass, a digital ad agency. While Snapchat makes money from advertising, Mr. Owens said, remaining relatively marketing-free will help the company differentiate itself.

All of this contrasts with how Facebook, Twitter and other social media networks have relied on celebrities and influencers to build the popularity of their services. Celebrity users were so important to Facebook when it went public in 2012 that the pages of Lady Gaga and an internet-famous dog named Boo were mentioned in the company's regulatory filings. Twitter's initial public offering filing in 2013 pointed out that the chef Mario Batali and President Obama were among its users.

Google's YouTube even helped create a new category of online celebrity — the influencer — by elevating popular video creators on the platform. And Instagram supports celebrities and influencers by sharing data that can help them attract larger audiences.

These moves have pushed many people to seek social media fame; some even try to make a living by selling products to their followers. These influencers have formed guilds, are supported by agents and are paid when they slip products into photos of themselves having fun and looking stylish.

Snapchat does not cater to these groups. Instead of having celebrities and influencers make product placements on the service, Snapchat tightly controls its ads, which must meet a high bar, according to advertisers. The ads are typically designed to mirror the look and the feel of videos and photos that users already see on the messaging service.

By keeping that quality control, Snapchat is able to charge a lot for its ads: $350,000 to $600,000 for a daylong national geofilter — a branded image that people can overlay on their photos — and up to $700,000 for so-called lenses that can transform a user's selfie, according to a price list obtained by The New York Times. The company recently introduced lower-priced advertising options.

Yet for a social media company to eschew celebrities and influencers is risky.

"You'd be crazy not to serve them well, because they represent a large amount of engagement and activity on most platforms," said

Michele Anderson, the chief operating officer of the media consulting firm Activate. To ignore influencers, she said, is a "shortsighted business risk."

Some online influencers have gone public with their displeasure over Snapchat's arm's-length approach. One of them, Shaun McBride, posted an 11-minute "open letter" to Snapchat on YouTube last month. In it, he complains about how poorly he says the company works with influencers and advertisers, and says it ignored his requests to be verified, a designation that indicates someone is a public figure whom others might try to impersonate. He calls Snapchat "cool but very expensive" for brands, and says that made it hard to build an audience.

"YouTube, I have a rep and they help me out with anything," Mr. McBride says in the video. "I've talked to people at Instagram about how Instagram stories work and we work together on stuff. Snapchat, I don't really have a point of contact, and they're not really embracing their creators."

In an email, Mr. McBride said his relationship with Snapchat did not change after he posted the video.

Snapchat is not celebrity-free. Apart from Mr. Sean, television personalities like Ryan Seacrest and musicians like Rihanna use the service. Last fall, the company rolled out "official stories," a feature that identifies videos and pictures posted by widely known public figures like Michelle Obama and Jessica Alba. Only a few hundred Snapchat accounts have the official story designation, which are marked with an emoji and are easier for users to find than regular accounts.

The tennis star Serena Williams became part of the official stories this year. She said she liked the upgrade because it "makes it easy for anyone to find me."

Yet celebrity accounts are not given other types of common preferential treatment. Their posts are not presented in a newsfeed, and an algorithm does not prioritize their content and automatically feed it to users. People must also choose to follow celebrity accounts and then opt to watch their stories. And Snapchat does not encourage celebrities to focus on metrics, nor does it reveal the number of followers a user has in the app.

"Snapchat isn't about the numbers," Ms. Williams said. "Snapchat is for my real fans."

The actor and comedian Kevin Hart, who has an official story account, also said the service gave him a more genuine connection with fans.

"Snapchat is where I go to connect with them in a fun, natural way," he said.

Arielle Vandenberg, an actress and social media star with more than 900,000 followers on Instagram, said she had found it hard at first to build a following on Snapchat. Still, she has started using the app more than any other.

"It feels like way more of a connection between me and the person who is watching," she said. "If I post a picture on Instagram, it could be taken two weeks ago. If I post on Snapchat, it's right there in the moment with the audience."

KATIE BENNER reported from San Francisco and **SAPNA MAHESHWARI** from New York.

We're Living in the World That Klout Built

OPINION | BY LIRIEL HIGA | MAY 14, 2018

Ms. Higa's Klout score is an unremarkable 50, down from a high of at least 65.

I THINK MY Klout score helped me get my first job working with Nicholas Kristof. In 2012, when I was interviewing to work with him, he mentioned my score on the site, which rates social media influence. It was high for a person who wasn't a well-known journalist, and he was huge on social media, so on the advice of a friend I included it on my résumé. He noticed, and we are now colleagues at The New York Times.

Now I cringe at the thought. It's like bragging about my high school G.P.A. When Klout announced last week that it was shutting down, it got an internet wake fueled by mocking from, of course, people with high Klout scores.

"I feel like this @Klout score should have gotten me into more parties," tweeted Anil Dash, an impressive 84 on a scale of 1 to 100.

Eve Peyser joked, "It's sad Klout is shutting down — what other service will congratulate me for being a gout expert?"

On May 25, Klout will shut down, but not because what it set out to do is irrelevant. On the contrary: Klout is closing because, well, we're living our Klout scores now. The "influencer economy" is thriving, and it has created a new vocabulary. *I just reached 500,000 Facebook fans! My YouTube video went viral. OMG, did you see who commented on my Instagram post? I'm trending worldwide. I checked in so many times I'm the mayor of my local bar.*

I was happy to get a professional boost from social media influence; today, entire careers are built on it. In our influencer-driven world, Kim Kardashian gets paid $500,000 for touting a product on Instagram. Product placement on social media is so rampant that

Olivia Wilde felt compelled to include the hashtag #notanad when she posted a picture of new sustainably made sneakers by Nike.

Perks aren't just for superstars. Alexandra Michelle (430,000 followers on Instagram) posts mesmerizing yoga videos and plugs the company that provides her apparel: "Outfit by my yoga fam @spiritualgangster." Laura Izumikawa shares photos and videos of her adorable daughter on Instagram, and on Mother's Day her 628,000 followers got a chance to win a bag, shoes and a necklace.

Aspiring influencers don't need to wait for companies to shower them with freebies or cash. On FameBit anyone with 5,000 subscribers or followers on YouTube, Twitter, Tumblr or Facebook can propose projects to sponsors across a variety of topics. And if companies don't have $500,000 for a plug from a Kardashian, they can go to Shoutcart, view social followings for thousands of lesser influencers and buy a shout-out for as little as $1.

Of course, there is a danger to all this. "Black Mirror," the science fiction television show, showed us what such a world looks like in the extreme. In the 2016 episode "Nosedive," people are constantly rated by friends, colleagues and even passers-by on the street. People whose score drops too low on the 5-point scale are barred from renting nice cars, rebooking flights and even entering the building in which they work.

Lacie Pound, our protagonist, is a solid 4.2 but aspires to move into a luxury apartment complex that gives discounts to 4.5's and above. Her plan to boost her score involves giving a knockout toast at a wedding, which has a guest list populated with high 4's. Being friendly to the barista isn't going to cut it; she needs people with high ratings to give her five stars.

But what seems like a parody is not so different from our world in 2018, and I'm not just talking about the challenge of getting a ride when you have a low Uber rating. A recent story in Wired about social ranking in China examined Zhima Credit, which doesn't just consider whether you pay your bills on time "but also what you buy, what degrees you hold, and the scores of your friends." Its chief executive was quoted as saying that Zhima Credit "will ensure that the bad people in society don't have a place to go, while good people can move freely and without obstruction."

I don't begrudge anyone their free workout gear. But I fear a world in which you could be denied freedom of movement because your best friends have blue-collar jobs or you never finished college.

In "Nosedive," the heroes are the ones who resist the pressure to be fake and conniving to achieve higher scores. At the end of the episode — spoiler alert! — Lacie's score has dropped to below one, she's in jail, and the technology embedded in her eyes that lets her see people's scores is removed. She gets into an argument with a fellow prisoner, and they start screaming at each other. But now, there's no need to choose their words carefully for fear of offending someone and getting a low rating. Freedom, at last.

LIRIEL HIGA is a staff editor in the Opinion section.

YouTube's Product Chief on Online Radicalization and Algorithmic Rabbit Holes

BY KEVIN ROOSE | MARCH 29, 2019

Neal Mohan discusses the streaming site's recommendation engine, which has become a growing liability amid accusations that it steers users to increasingly extreme content.

IT'S BEEN CALLED "one of the most powerful radicalizing instruments of the 21st century," "a petri dish of divisive, conspiratorial and sometimes hateful content," and a tool that "drives people to the internet's darkest corners."

I'm talking, of course, about YouTube — and, specifically, the recommendation algorithm that determines which videos the site plays after the one you're watching. That algorithm is YouTube's beating heart, keeping users hooked to the platform for hours on end. (The company has said recommendations are responsible for about 70 percent of the total time users spend on the site.)

The recommendation engine is also a growing liability for YouTube, which has been accused of steering users toward increasingly extreme content. After the recent mass shooting in Christchurch, New Zealand — the work of a gunman who showed signs of having been radicalized online — critics asked whether YouTube and other platforms were not just allowing hateful and violent content to exist but actively promoting it to their users. YouTube's biggest competitor, Facebook, said last week that it would ban white nationalism and white separatism on its platforms.

I recently spoke with Neal Mohan, YouTube's chief product officer, about criticism of the company's algorithms and what it is doing to address radicalization and violent extremism on the platform. We spoke about the things YouTube has already done to rein in extreme content — hiring additional reviewers, introducing a "breaking news shelf" that kicks in after major news events, altering the recommendation algorithm to reduce the distribution of conspiracy theories and other "borderline content" — and about the company's plans for the future.

The conversation was edited for length and clarity.

Q. *I'm wondering what you think about the conversation happening around radicalization on YouTube.*

A. I think some of it has to do with the fact that, as you know and as you've written about, YouTube was started as, and remains, an open platform for content and voices and opinions and thoughts. Many of them being, you know, really across the entire spectrum, many of which you or I or others may or may not agree with. I wouldn't be at YouTube, working on what I work on, if I didn't believe in the power of diversity of voices and opinions.

Having said that, we do take this notion of dissemination of harmful misinformation, hate-filled content, content that in some cases is inciting violence, extremely seriously.

Q. *I hear a lot about the "rabbit hole" effect, where you start watching one video and you get nudged with recommendations toward a slightly more sort of extreme video, and so on, and all of a sudden you're watching something really extreme. Is that a real phenomenon?*

A. Yeah, so I've heard this before, and I think that there are some myths that go into that description that I think it would be useful for me to debunk.

The first is this notion that it's somehow in our interests for the recommendations to shift people in this direction because it boosts watch time or what have you. I can say categorically that's not the way that our recommendation systems are designed. Watch time is one signal that they use, but they use a number of other engagement and satisfaction signals from the user. It is not the case that "extreme" content drives a higher version of engagement or watch time than content of other types.

I can also say that it's not in our business interest to promote any of this sort of content. It's not something that has a disproportionate effect in terms of watch time. Just as importantly, the watch time that it does generate doesn't monetize, because advertisers many times don't want to be associated with this sort of content.

And so the idea that it has anything to do with our business interests, I think it's just purely a myth.

Q. *So, why do people talk about this rabbit hole effect — you know, I went to watch one video about President Trump and now I'm just getting a stream of recommendations of increasingly more partisan content. Why do you think there's this perception that this is what happens on YouTube?*

A. This is one of the things that we looked at closely as we were developing the technology that went into that recommendation change that I described to you from a few weeks back.

We really looked at this to see what was happening on those "watch next" panels, in terms of the videos that were being recommended. And the first thing that I should say is that when we make recommendations after a video has been consumed, we don't take into account any notion of whether that's less or more extreme.

So when we looked at the data, we saw that a lot of the videos that were being recommended, as you would expect, had to do with the context of the video that was being consumed. That's obviously no surprise, but the videos that you saw on the panel, there were videos that you might consider to be maybe a little bit more extreme than what you had just consumed.

But you'll also see videos that were less extreme, or that you could call more toward the quote-unquote mainstream. It's equally — depending on a user's behavior — likely that you could have started on a more extreme video and actually moved in the other direction.

That's what our research showed when we were looking at this more closely. Now, that doesn't mean that we don't want to address what we talked about, which is just —

Q. *Sorry, can I just interrupt you there for a second? Just let me be clear: You're saying that there is no rabbit hole effect on YouTube?*

A. What I'm saying is that when a video is watched, you will see a number of videos that are then recommended. Some of those videos might have the perception of skewing in one direction or, you know, call it more extreme. There are other videos that skew in the opposite direction. And again, our systems are not doing this, because that's not a signal that feeds into the recommendations. That's just the observation that you see in the panel.

I'm not saying that a user couldn't click on one of those videos that are quote-unquote more extreme, consume that and then get another set of recommendations and sort of keep moving in one path or the other. All I'm saying is that it's not inevitable.

Q. *In the case of breaking news, you guys made a decision that showing authoritative information to people who were looking for it was important enough to radically shift the way recommendations and search results work, by moving to an approved or "authoritative sources" model rather than using the regular recommendation algorithm. Why not do that for everything?*

A. Let me say a few things about that. The first is that using a combination of those tools of authoritative content and promoting authoritative content is something that can apply to other information verticals, not just breaking news.

Having said that, as you continue to broaden the application of something like that, it's quite a blunt hammer. And so it does come with trade-offs. For example, how do you define something authoritative across the broad swath of YouTube when many of the use cases, as you know, are outside of the information-seeking realm? They're entertainment, they're oftentimes driven by people's personal tastes, like music and comedy and the like.

Q. *Right, but you could do it just for politics, hypothetically, and say that for any political video, we're going to move to this "authoritative sources" model.*

A. I think that even when you go to something that broad, it comes with real trade-offs. And I'm just raising the fact that there are considerations there, which is that you are then limiting political discourse to a set of preordained voices and outlets and publications. And I think that especially when it comes to something as charged and societally impactful as politics, there needs to be room for new voices to be heard.

Q. *Since the New Zealand shooting, we've heard this question about "Well, the platforms worked together to take down ISIS content. Why haven't they done the same for white supremacy or violent right-wing extremism?" What's the answer there?*

A. The first thing that I would say, just as a matter of fact, is that there were two sets of challenges when it came to the New Zealand shooting. One was everything that we just talked about in terms of surfacing authoritative, high-quality information — not showing, you know, conspiracies or harmful misinformation. That was one bucket.

The other bucket had to do with the velocity at which re-uploads were coming to these various platforms, and that is an area where we collaborated. We worked closely with other platforms in terms of making sure we had fingerprints of these videos, just like they did, and we shared those.

The other thing I would say, just more generally, in the case of violent extremism and limiting those videos on the platform, the reason it's different than what we're talking about here is that those [ISIS] videos took on a particular form. They were often designed for propaganda purposes and recruitment purposes. So they had things like branding and logos, both visually and in terms of the music they might use. Those formed a set of finite clues we could use to bring that content down. And, of course, we collaborated with other platforms to do that.

In the case of something like this, the challenges are harder because the line, as you can imagine, is sometimes blurry between what clearly might be hate speech versus what might be political speech that we might find distasteful and disagree with, but nonetheless is coming from, you know, candidates that are in elections and the like.

Q. *So much of what YouTube has become over the years is this kind of alternative form of media. People don't go to YouTube because they want the same stuff they would see on TV. They go because they've built relationships with creators that they trust, and when Logan Paul puts out a flat-earth documentary or Shane Dawson questions whether 9/11 happened, there's a sense that YouTube is the place where these "real" explanations are being offered, and maybe that makes this all very hard to undo.*

A. There's nearly two billion people that come to our platform every month. Every one of them is coming for some unique reason, whether it's the latest and greatest music video or a YouTube original, or their favorite creators.

I think when people come to YouTube looking for information, it has resulted in a shift in the way that we think about the responsibility of our platform. As a result of that shift, our product teams here are thinking of all of these solutions, many of which we've talked about here, as a means of addressing that responsibility for making sure that when users are looking for information, YouTube is putting its best foot forward in terms of serving that information to them. But YouTube is also still keeping users in power, in terms of their intent and the information that they're looking for.

It's an ongoing effort. I think we've made great strides here. But clearly there's more work to be done.

What if Instagram Got Rid of Likes?

BY JOHN HERRMAN | MAY 31, 2019

Social networks built on public status markers are now starting to hide them.

IN LATE APRIL, at F8, Facebook's annual event for developers, the company's head of Instagram, Adam Mosseri, announced some updates. Plenty of things would be added to the photo-sharing app: new ways to post Stories, new ways to buy stuff, an updated camera. Some things might also be taken away. Follower counts, Instagram's main status marker, would become "much less prominent" in users' profiles. "A bigger idea," he told the gathered crowd, was "private like counts," meaning no more numbers under your friends' posts.

Earlier that month, during an interview at a TED conference, the Twitter chief executive Jack Dorsey shared a big idea of his own. "If I had to start the service again, I would not emphasize the follower count as much," he said. "I would not emphasize the 'like' count as much. I don't think I would even create 'like' in the first place." A few weeks later, in a post on its community blog, YouTube announced a small but notable change to the way it would display subscriber counts on channels — in more cases, the company said, numbers would be rounded.

Following years of increasing scrutiny, leaders at each company seem to be gathering around the same small solution: adjusting or eliminating metrics. This would represent a notable turn for services so strongly identified with public, comparable and newly valuable numbers. It also raises the question: If this is their solution, what do these people think is the problem?

INFLUENCE AS PUBLIC HEALTH CRISIS

"We don't want Instagram to feel like a competition," Mr. Mosseri said at F8. Instagram, he hoped, would become "a space that feels much less pressurized." Mr. Dorsey's word for Twitter's dilemma was "toxicity," which he thought could be decreased if big, bold numbers weren't providing "incentives" for the wrong things. YouTube said that its change was simply a matter of ensuring numbers are displayed consistently across the service; in recent months, however, the company has dealt with a series of consuming and highly public feuds between creators, each involving follower counts — increasing, decreasing, competing — in central ways.

That Instagram can feel "pressurized" and trigger status anxiety is hard to dispute; even Twitter's most satisfied customers would admit that it can become "toxic." But to conclude that these men are merely late to engage with the most obvious (and obviously correct) of their users' critiques would be a misunderstanding. Their problems aren't our problems. Their job, as ever, is to get people to use the services. Metrics helped them do this job for a while, showing new users what to aim for and then reminding them constantly what success looks like. This was during the growth phase, for both users and the new platforms they were joining. Their priorities seemed aligned. Now, that era is passing.

In 2019, by most measures except its stock price, Twitter is conspicuously stagnant. Follower counts do not necessarily translate to people actually engaging with posts; it's not uncommon, for example, to see a brand with hundreds of thousands of followers post updates that receive virtually no human interactions. (The company recently did away with another metric: It will no longer report its "monthly active user" metric to investors, instead emphasizing a new one that may tell a more favorable story: "monetizable daily active users.")

Instagram may be the pride of Facebook, and it's still growing briskly overall, according to the company. One problem suggested, and answered, by hiding likes is that people aren't posting to their feeds as much as they used to. Instead, they're posting Stories, the transient format copied from Snapchat. Removing a metric from beneath regular Instagram posts *might* alleviate some stress among users; it would also help minimize the sense that the thing that first made Instagram popular is in decline.

ERIK CARTER

The real problem, from Instagram's perspective, is the kind of thing you might worry about if you were clearly "incentivized" by metrics of an internal, top-level variety: not that Instagram isn't growing, or that people aren't using it, but that maybe they're using one part of it less, when they should be using all of it more.

NETWORKS MINUS NUMBERS

What would a metric-free, or metric-light, social media actually feel like? It's not so easy to imagine revisionist platform histories, given how integral metrics have been to the stories of their rapid rise and dominance. These omnipresent numbers have also served as imperfect but widely used ways to quantify revolutions, jokes, screw-ups and presidencies. And their proprietary and borrowed names — shares, likes, follows, views — have infused our everyday speech.

In earlier incarnations, both Twitter and Instagram presented users with simple chronological feeds, and visible metrics also provided secondary sorting mechanics. These numbers — how many people liked something, or commented on something, or re-shared something, or followed someone — were a biased, ruthless and explicit value system. That these numbers were goals unto themselves was implied from the start.

Instagram without quantified likes might have been *nicer*, in some way. But it would not have produced the Instagram we know today, and certainly not the Instagram purchased by Facebook for a billion dollars, which became the Instagram of influencers, which is the Instagram of status anxiety, which is the Instagram of more than a billion users.

Looking forward, though, a nearly number-free social media is somewhat easier to visualize. If you primarily consume Instagram Stories, you're already seeing one version of it. And today, what you see on Twitter and Instagram already depends on a mixture of signals — things you've liked in the past, how much time you've spent looking at a particular user's content, whether you communicate privately with a given user and whether you have an affinity for some topic or another — not just chronology, likes or retweets. Those signals are all metrics too, of a sort, invisible to us but very much legible to the platforms themselves. Imagine a ticker in your Instagram app counting up the number of times you've scrolled, or tallying the number of times you've tapped, or counting up the seconds you've spent looking at an image. These *already exist*, somewhere, and may inform what you see every day. They're just not for you to know.

Understood this way, the idea that metrics are the problem sounds an awful lot like these companies saying their users can no longer be trusted, not even with the scraps of actionable data they've been allowed to see for years. (It also doubles as a way to share the premise that there must be a healthy *and* highly monetizable way to use these services, and that the platforms can be trusted to figure out what it is.) These metrics have outlived their original purpose and been assigned new roles behind the scenes. (TikTok, a much newer app still in its early period of frantic growth, lavishes users with metrics and feedback, and it works. We haven't changed; our apps have.)

Likes and retweets used to be translated into signals for people. Now they just provide signals for the machines. In the newer, less immediately comprehensible versions of our feeds, where what we see is chosen according to processes that we can only guess at, Twitter and Instagram suggest the existence of dozens of metrics that are hidden by default. If our feeds are already assembled based on cues from countless secret metrics, why not hide a couple more?

The response to Instagram's announcement has been muted, aside from some panic among professional influencers. The company tested the change in Canada, where some users received a message explaining the change: "We want your followers to focus on what you share, not how many likes your posts get." Whether the company rolls it out further remains to be seen. (For some users, the test has already ended.) Likewise, the relationship between things Jack Dorsey thinks are interesting at the time and actual features in the Twitter platform is, at best, extremely loose.

At YouTube, though, where the change was real but much smaller — rounded numbers of followers instead of exact numbers, making small directional fluctuations harder to detect and, say, make into the subject of a video — the response was harsh. The daily experience of using Instagram and Twitter over the last few years has given users the impression that the few visible metrics are, if not unimportant, at least somewhat devalued and decoupled from one another, and from reality. Power and clout gained on the platforms is largely expressed and monetized through third parties, as with influencers, or manifested elsewhere, in, say, politics.

On YouTube, followers and video views translate directly into payment from the company. "No one wants this," wrote one of hundreds of users responding to the company's announcement. "People who keep their sub counts public want to show the full number." Another explained why. "Time could be better spent fixing problems that users have reported across the site, not abbreviating sub counts, which can lead to lost potential business opportunities," the user wrote. "Why do you hate your content creators so much?" asked another.

Melodramatic as they may sound, these responses reflect a rational understanding of what YouTube is, and what any social network is, really: a marketplace with goods and currency and winners and losers, governed by an all-powerful and unaccountable corporation. Metrics mean money, and knowing them provides a rare if fleeting sense of knowledge and control in an environment otherwise ruled by secrets — one that will exploit you whether or not you actively try to exploit *it*. For users, numbers are power. For the platforms, so is hiding them.

JOHN HERRMAN covers tech and media for the Times Magazine, and was one of the first three recipients of The Times's David Carr Fellowship. Previously, he was a reporter for the Business section.

CHAPTER 4

International Influencers

Social media may have its beginning in many American companies, but its reach extends worldwide. However, many countries seek to limit the free exchange of ideas among their citizens. China has exerted considerable control over their population in an attempt to censor the social media they consume. Dangers exist for influencers in countries as diverse as Cuba and Pakistan — dangers that can turn lethal. Shocking acts of violence such as the 2019 New Zealand mosque murders reveal a dark side to the influence of social media: The killer not only live-streamed the murders on Facebook, but he encouraged people to subscribe to PewDiePie, one of YouTube's biggest stars.

Where an Internet Joke Is Not Just a Joke

BY BROOK LARMER | OCT. 26, 2011

THE CELLPHONE VIBRATED softly, insistently, echoing off the whitewashed walls of the artist's studio. It was a Sunday morning in early April, and Wang Bo — an Internet animator better known to his legions of online fans by his nickname, Pi San — ignored the call at first. He wanted no intrusions. A compact 40-year-old with short-cropped hair and arched eyebrows that give him a look of permanent bemusement, Pi San is most famous for creating a mischievous cartoon character named Kuang Kuang, but he earns money by making animations for corporations, and he was on a deadline. Pi San had bicycled to his studio in a defunct factory building on the outskirts of Beijing that morning, hoping to finish up some work in peace. But the buzzing of the phone didn't stop.

The moment Pi San picked up, the caller blurted out the news: State security agents had just detained Ai Weiwei, China's most famous contemporary artist and a government critic. Pi San spat out a profanity. Over the previous six weeks, hundreds of bloggers — lawyers, activists, journalists — had vanished into police custody in one of the harshest assaults on social activism in decades. Now they had Ai — fat, brilliant, bombastic and internationally renowned. If Ai could be arrested, was any independent thinker in China safe?

Pi San had reason to be scared. He and Ai were friends. A few weeks earlier, over lunch, the two artists talked about collaborating on a satirical Internet animation. Though a bit wary of Ai's Web activism, Pi San admired his daring solo exhibitions in New York, Berlin and London. The most recent show had consisted of 100 million sunflower seeds made of porcelain, laid out across the floor of the Tate Modern, which visitors were invited to walk upon. Some considered the seeds to be symbols of the downtrodden Chinese people.

Despite his fear, Pi San quickly posted the news about Ai's detention on Sina Weibo, China's closely monitored equivalent of Twitter and the fastest-growing Internet platform in the world. An invisible censor deleted the message in seconds. He then tried posting, without comment, a cartoon drawing of Ai, the better to evade China's word-sensitive filtering software. But the image disappeared, too — a sign that a human being, not computer software, had deleted the drawing. Pi San told his Weibo followers: "Again I was 'harmonized.' It's just a picture!"

Now the creative synapses started firing. "I had to do something to lift the fear," Pi San told me later. "Others might write or protest; I make animations." He and a colleague worked feverishly through the night on a 54-second flash animation entitled "Crack Sunflower Seeds." The animation takes place in Kuang Kuang's school, where a little girl is speaking over the loudspeakers. "Once upon a time," she begins, "there was a Chinese man selling sunflower seeds." Suddenly, a black cartoon hand yanks her off the set. A succession of trembling announcers tries to tell the same story, but the black hand pulls them off too, each time more quickly than the last.

Finally, it is Kuang Kuang's turn. The boy hems and haws and, giving up, sighs in exasperation: "Ai." A word bubble appears with the Chinese character for the sigh (哎), virtually the same as Ai's surname (艾). Kuang Kuang is hauled off, screaming. In the next frame, the black hand sweeps away sunflower seeds arranged in the same "Ai." Then we hear a grating sound — teeth meeting porcelain — followed by an off-screen scream: "Damn it! Who sold us these fake sunflower seeds?"

Pi San finished the animation before dawn on April 4, less than 24 hours after Ai was detained. "I hesitated for a second before posting it online," he told me. "But then I thought, If I don't put it up, that would be like self-castration." With a few clicks, he sent "Crack Sunflower Seeds" into cyberspace, posting it onto China's top video Web sites. In just a few hours, a million or more netizens watched the animation online. Then the video began disappearing from Chinese Web sites one by one, just like the announcers in his animation. Pi San lashed out directly at the censors in a Weibo post: "You're like the eunuch who gets worried before the emperor does!" There was no response. Even in his anger, Pi San was left wondering if the black hand would come for him.

No government in the world pours more resources into patrolling the Web than China's, tracking down unwanted content and supposed miscreants among the online population of 500 million with an army of more than 50,000 censors and vast networks of advanced filtering software. Yet despite these restrictions — or precisely because of them — the Internet is flourishing as the wittiest space in China. "Censorship warps us in many ways, but it is also the mother of creativity," says Hu Yong, an Internet expert and associate professor at Peking University. "It forces people to invent indirect ways to get their meaning across, and humor works as a natural form of encryption."

To slip past censors, Chinese bloggers have become masters of comic subterfuge, cloaking their messages in protective layers of irony and satire. This is not a new concept, but it has erupted so powerfully that it now defines the ethos of the Internet in China. Coded language has become part of mainstream culture, with the most contagious memes tapping into widely shared feelings about issues that cannot be openly discussed, from corruption and economic inequality to censorship itself. "Beyond its comic value, this humor shows where netizens are pushing against the boundaries of the state," says Xiao Qiang, an adjunct professor at the University of California, Berkeley, whose Web site, China Digital Times, maintains an entertaining lexicon of coded Internet terms. "Nothing else gives us a clearer view of the pressure points in Chinese society."

So pervasive is this irreverent subculture that the Chinese have a name for it: *egao*, meaning "evil works" or, more roughly, "mischievous mockery." In its simplest form, *egao* (pronounced "EUH-gow") lampoons the powerful without being overtly rebellious. President Hu Jintao's favorite buzz word, "harmony," which he deploys constantly when urging social stability, is hijacked to signify censorship itself, as in, "My blog's been harmonized." June 4, the censored date of the 1989 massacre of pro-democracy protesters, is rendered as May 35 — or "535." There are also more complex forms of *egao*, like Hu Ge's 2010 film spoof, "Animal World," in which a rare species of Internet users is "saved" from "compulsive thinking disorder," i.e., the urge to think freely.

Satire is sometimes a safety valve that government might grudgingly permit. Better a virtual laugh, after all, than a real protest. But being laughed at, as Orwell found during his stint as a colonial police officer in Burma, can also be a ruler's greatest fear. And the Chinese government, which last year sentenced a woman to a year of hard labor for a sarcastic three-word tweet, appears to suffer from an acute case of humor deficiency. "Jokes that mock the abuse of power do more than let off steam; they mobilize people's emotions," says Wen Yunchao, an outspoken blogger who often mounts sardonic Internet campaigns in defense of free speech. "Every time a joke takes off," Wen says, "it chips away at the so-called authority of an authoritarian regime."

Satirical threads sweeping across the Internet can often seem like brush fires whose origins are lost in the conflagration. But behind every outbreak are individuals probing the limits of self-expression, flirting, often perilously, with the blurry line between the permissible and the punishable. Over the past several months I followed two individuals — the animator Pi San and the blogger Wen Yunchao — in an effort to understand the dynamics of "mischievous mockery" and the increasingly serious game of cat-and-mouse taking place along China's digital front lines.

Pi San and Wen are perfect counterpoints — a northerner and a southerner who approach egao from different angles. One specializes in visual images, the other mainly in words. Pi San shudders at being considered an activist; he sees satire as an artistic way to vent personal frustration. Wen wears the activist label proudly; he views humor as a "weapon of the weak" to mobilize civil society. As the government crackdown intensified, each man was forced to adjust his calculations of danger and opportunity: How far could they go before they crossed the invisible line?

Wen learned the true power of Internet humor not from a joke but from a cry for help from a police interrogation room. Early one morning in July 2009, Wen, who is 39, woke up in his apartment in the southern city of Guangzhou to find a startling message on his Twitter feed: "I have been arrested by Mawei police, SOS." The jailhouse tweet was from Guo Baofeng, a young friend and fellow blogger, referring to a district in the coastal city Xiamen, some 300 miles away. Minutes later came another tweet from Guo, also in English: "Pls help me, I grasped the phone during police sleep."

Then there was nothing.

Wen knew how easily people could disappear into the labyrinths of China's prison system. Guo, who was then a 25-year-old English-language translator, had reposted a video in which the mother of a gang-raped murder victim accused local Xiamen authorities of a cover-up. Now Wen wondered how far the police would go to muzzle the messenger.

The tweets from detention — and the silence that followed — unsettled Wen. But what could he do? Any direct protest would be shut down immediately, even if people could overcome their fear to participate. Then he noticed a phrase that was going viral on the Internet: "Jia Junpeng, your mother is calling you home for dinner!"

The line's origins were a mystery, but the online masses latched onto it as a joking commentary on their Web-addicted generation — lost in cyberspace, unreachable by the outside world. That very day, millions retweeted the phrase. Wen, though, gave it a new twist. He urged his tens of thousands of microblog followers to send postcards to the Mawei police station and post photos of them online, all with the same words: "Guo Baofeng, your mother is calling you home for dinner!"

Nobody can know if the Internet campaign made a difference. But instead of being lost in the prison system — four other bloggers arrested for reposting the same video were sentenced to one to two years in prison — Guo was released after 16 days. For Wen, the incident crystallized his thinking. "Humor can amplify the power of the social media," he told me. "If it hits a nerve, like a case of injustice or abuse, it can be contagious. It's indirect — just a joke, right? — so people lose their fear of getting involved."

Growing up as the oldest child in a poor family in rural Guangdong Province, Wen wasn't always keen to get involved himself. When army tanks crushed the 1989 pro-democracy movement in Beijing, Wen, who was then a middle-school student prone to skipping class, applauded the crackdown. "I agreed with the government that it was necessary to prevent chaos," he recalls. Wen's most daring act in college — he was assigned to study machine welding at a technical institute in Harbin, a city in China's icy far north — was to smuggle in Cantonese pornography and pop music to help him endure the long winters.

His Internet "awakening," as he calls it, came years later, when he toiled at a power station near Guangzhou. One night after clocking out, Wen watched a television special beamed in from nearby Hong Kong that contradicted the official story of the 1989 massacre. Finding a trove of information online to confirm its veracity — this was before the Great Firewall, erected in 2003, blocked such terms as "June 4" — he emerged with a new conviction: "The Internet will open the door of democracy."

Hungry to learn more, Wen transformed himself over the next decade into an information machine, first as a journalist and then as a blogger. Covering events for state-run newspapers and, later, for government television, he produced reports and commentaries that toed the official line. On the Internet, though, he adopted a more freewheeling persona, writing a popular blog called Ramblings of a Drunkard under a pseudonym. Soon, Wen moved full time online, working for the Chinese Internet company Netease and moonlighting as one of the country's earliest citizen journalists. His first article, typed into his cellphone, chronicled the 2007 street protests in Xiamen that succeeded in halting construction of a chemical plant.

The censors were never far behind, turning Wen's life into a perpetual game of hide-and-seek. First a few posts were blocked, then his entire blog, then the Chinese Internet portal he used. An overseas Web server worked until the Great Firewall shut it out too. Riding the next wave of technology, Wen began typing out 140-character blasts on Twitter and China's fast-growing microblogging sites. Weibo, a Twitter equivalent that barely existed two years ago, now has 200 million users, churning out some 40 million messages a day. The government, hard-pressed to keep up, leans on Web companies to censor their own content in return for "self-discipline" points needed to renew licenses. "No place is safe anymore," Wen says. "But whenever censorship grows, so do the opportunities for sarcasm and satire."

Not long ago, Wen even dared to target China's most unassailable icon: Mao Zedong. The chairman has been dead for 35 years, but his massive portrait still presides over Tiananmen Square. It is just one sign of what Wen calls the "awful influence" wielded by the founder of the People's Republic. Ridiculing Mao is almost unthinkable in China today. Even so, on the anniversary of Mao's death in 2009, Wen urged his online followers to join a devious "de-Maoification" campaign. Since "mao" is also the Chinese word for "hair," he suggested posting before-and-after shots of shaved body parts — people literally "getting rid of mao."

Wen is a beer-bellied man with a thick Abraham Lincoln-style beard. Among the hundreds of images of shorn beards and hair-free legs that flashed across the Web that day was Wen's own contribution: a photo of his rotund belly with its hair in a topiary of the "t" of the Twitter logo. Wen's abdominal salute was funny, but it was also a manifesto for a more open China — and a dangerous move in his showdown with Chinese authorities.

When Pi San was a young boy — around the same age as his impish creation, Kuang Kuang — his parents used to smack his hand with a ruler every time they caught him drawing cartoons in the margins of his school books. "I was a mediocre student," says Pi San, whose family lived in a bleak copper-mining town in the hills of Shanxi Province. "My parents thought my doodling doomed me to a life in the mine."

Despite the punishment, Pi San kept drawing, even selling caricatures of Kung Fu heroes to his friends. Nearly two decades later, Pi San runs Hutoon, the animation company he founded in 2005. Hutoon's staff of 50 young designers fills most of a floor in "798," a trendy district of art galleries, studios and cafes built on the remnants of a military electronics factory in northeastern Beijing. The young men and women — most dressed in black, like their boss — huddle over banks of computers, the clicketyclack of keyboards resounding in the high-ceilinged industrial space.

When I first visited his fourth-floor studio in early March, Pi San seemed to move easily between his roles as entrepreneur and provocateur, a reflection of what he jokingly calls his multiple-personality disorder. A few years ago, Hutoon produced an animated series for China Central Television — the government's main propaganda arm — but Pi San chafed at the lack of creative freedom. "Even CCTV's cartoons are all about indoctrination, not entertainment," he said. Now he and his staff crank out animated Internet ads and videos for clients including rock stars and Fortune 500 firms like Motorola and Samsung.

In mid-April, I watched Pi San and his crew work on an episode of "Ms. Puff," Hutoon's most lucrative animation series. Centered on a risqué but apolitical female character — censors notice Puff only when the strap on her camisole slips — the series is the first original animated content commissioned by Youku, the Chinese equivalent of YouTube. Two weeks earlier, Youku had been one of the first Web sites to delete his anti-censorship satire, "Crack Sunflower Seeds." This didn't matter to Pi San. Hutoon's financial future depended on the success of "Ms. Puff." "You have to have a split personality to succeed in China," he told me. "With some animations, I make money. With others, I just make fun."

That afternoon, though, the boss was preoccupied. There was no news of Ai Weiwei, and Pi San's thoughts about the future — that of his wife and their 7-year-old son — cycled between anger, fear and resignation. Leaving Hutoon's main studio, he led me to a back room filled with heaps of corrugated cardboard, which were the miniature sets used in the Kuang Kuang animations. "This is where I come when my emotions are running high," Pi San said, bending down to examine the eight-inch-tall room that loomed large in "Crack Sunflower Seeds."

Nearby was a tiny school building featured in Pi San's first Kuang Kuang satire in 2009, a mordant swipe at the education system called "Blow Up the School." An instant Internet sensation among Chinese youth, the animation generated a few million hits on its first day and so angered officials that they slapped him with a fine for "inappropriate content." As more irreverent Kuang Kuang videos appeared, Internet fan clubs formed in nearly every Chinese province, turning the bubble-headed boy and his creator into minor cult figures.

None of Pi San's work has evoked China's social ills more provocatively than "Little Rabbit, Be Good," made last January. The four-minute "greeting card" to mark the Chinese Year of the Rabbit begins as a soothing bedtime story about bunny rabbits. But as Kuang Kuang drifts off to sleep, the story morphs into a nightmare. Ruled by tigers (the outgoing zodiac sign) who promise to "build a harmonious forest" — a pointed jab at Hu Jintao's catchphrase — the rabbits suffer an endless series of abuses. Babies die from drinking poisoned milk. A protester fighting forced eviction gets crushed under a tiger's car. A reckless driver kills a rabbit in a hit-and-run and boasts about his high-level police protection.

The thinly disguised allegory is based on real-life events that sparked outrage on the Internet. The ending, however, is sheer fantasy. Instead of accepting their fate, the rabbits rise up in revolt, ripping their tiger overlords apart with their bare teeth in a catharsis of "South Park"-style violence. The uprising ends with a warning: "Even rabbits bite when they are pushed."

Pi San knew "Little Rabbit" might have crossed the line. After consulting a fortuneteller — "I wanted to know if this would cause me trouble," he said — he hedged his bets, uploading the video to a few small fan Web sites in the middle of the night. "Little Rabbit" still received more than 70,000 hits within two hours, he says. By the time censors deleted the versions proliferating across the Internet two days later, an estimated three to four million people had seen it. Local media didn't touch the story, but foreign journalists pressed him on the video's political message. His coy response: "I only made a fairy tale."

Pi San's dark satire landed just as popular revolutions fueled by social media in Tunisia and Egypt were beginning to topple dictators. A few weeks later, Chinese bloggers who alluded online to the possibilities of a similar "jasmine" revolution in China would be detained. "I was worried," Pi San admitted. "The line moves all the time, so we never know where we stand."

Most Chinese Internet users don't give the invisible line between acceptable satire and detainable offense a second thought. They may know it exists, but their online activities — shopping, blogging, gaming, networking — remain safely within the confines of the Great Firewall. But the boundary is of the utmost concern for a growing number of artists and activists. "The government's primary means of control is the fuzzy line," says David Bandurski, a researcher at the China Media Project at Hong Kong University. "No one ever knows exactly where the line is. The control apparatus is built on uncertainty and self-censorship, on creating this atmosphere of fear."

Wen felt the line shift a year ago, after judges in Oslo awarded the Nobel Peace Prize to the jailed Chinese writer Liu Xiaobo. Few Chinese had ever heard of the man behind Charter 08, the human-rights declaration that, like Liu's name, was banned inside the Great Firewall. But the government was apoplectic. Chinese officials smeared the "criminal" Liu in the press, pressured foreign countries to boycott the ceremony and blocked a raft of new words on the Internet, even "Norway" and "Nobel."

When the banned words extended to the phrase "empty chair" — the most conspicuous sign of Liu's absence at the Nobel ceremony — Wen hit on an idea. If the words were not allowed, why not post photos of empty chairs as a tribute to Liu? "Everyone has an empty chair," Wen pleaded with his 40,000-plus followers on Twitter and Weibo. "If we only watch, then one day [the empty chair] might appear by your family's dining table as well." At his urging, bloggers posted dozens of seemingly innocuous pictures online, from an empty chair in a Van Gogh painting to a magazine ad for an Ikea lounger. The censors eventually caught on to the joke, but not before Wen had turned a bit of microblog mischief into a human rights statement.

Three months later came the broad crackdown seeming to stem from Beijing's paranoia about the possible domestic repercussions from the uprisings in the Middle East and North Africa. Wen was visiting Hong Kong when he received an e-mail warning from Chinese public-security agents: "Don't come home. You'll be arrested before you even see your wife and son." His was now the empty chair. Wen decided to wait out the threats in Hong Kong, which is governed by different laws than the rest of China. Wen's absence may have spared him detention or prison, but now he was in limbo.

When I visited Wen in Hong Kong in April, he was living in a temporary apartment with a row of shirts drip-drying in the window. Dinner consisted of a six-pack of beer followed by sausages fried up at 1 a.m. At one point, he pulled out his BlackBerry. "Gone, gone, gone," Wen said, as he scrolled down a list of friends who had vanished, most likely into police custody.

Wen's Twitter account was now swarming with the gadflies of the 50-Cent Party, which is the nickname for commentators who reportedly get paid 50 Chinese cents for every pro-government post. He showed me the barrage of disparaging tweets he had received, along with two fake Twitter accounts the 50-Centers had set up to look like his. More menacing were the text warnings from anonymous senders who seemed to know everything about him: his identification number, his travel itineraries, even details about his wife, his 10-year-old son and his parents.

Early in the evening, Wen scoffed at the intimidation attempts. "The government has too much invested in the Internet financially to shut it down, so all it can do is resort to scare tactics," he said. But as the night wore on and the beer cans piled up, he confided: "I'm worried they might pick me up even here in Hong Kong. I'm even more frightened for my family."

The following day, I joined Wen on an excursion to Lingnan University, along Hong Kong's border with mainland China, where he was to give a talk about Internet activism. On the train ride out, he spoke about his tenuous life in Hong Kong. A local satellite television company had hired him to develop a show that would beam propaganda-free reports into China. At night, Wen still tweeted prodigiously, launching jokes and spoofs over the Great Firewall, like a medieval catapulter outside the castle ramparts. His wife and son would join him in Hong Kong months later, but Wen's inability to return freely to his homeland left him depressed. “I got angry the other day when a friend called me a *liuwang*, an exile,” he told me. “It’s such a sad word. I never thought it would apply to me.” At the university that evening, a table covered in red velvet had been set up on a small outdoor stage. Wen was handed a microphone, but it proved unnecessary. Fewer than a dozen students stopped to listen. The train home skirted within a few hundred yards of the mainland Chinese border. Hurtling through the darkness, Wen looked up from his BlackBerry and gazed out toward the border, the one line he may never cross again.

As a cocoon of heat and smog enveloped Beijing last June, Pi San began to wilt. Two months had passed since Ai Weiwei was detained, and the artist’s fate and whereabouts were still unknown. The police had also detained another close friend of Pi San’s, the rock musician Zuoxiao Zuzhou, just days after a live performance in which the words “Free Ai Weiwei!” appeared on a giant screen above him. The musician was released within a day, but Pi San was spooked. He shelved an idea for another Kuang Kuang satire and began, for the first time, to consider seriously his friends’ advice to leave the country.

Then, on June 22, came a surprise: Ai reappeared at his home after 81 days in detention. The artist provocateur, much thinner now, was uncharacteristically silent. Though not formally charged with a crime, he was still under a form of house arrest “pending further investigation” into tax fraud. Two days later, Pi San rode his electric bicycle to the blue door of Ai’s studio — “like a delivery boy,” he said. High-spirited as ever, Ai marched back and forth across the small room, showing Pi San how he had lost so much weight. The two friends talked for hours. Given Ai’s house arrest, their plan to collaborate on a satirical animation would have to wait. When Pi San was about to leave, Ai gave him a memento from his days in custody: a couple of stale biscuits, part of his “detention diet.”

Many artists and bloggers interpreted Ai’s release as merely a face-saving measure to help Premier Wen Jiabao avoid embarrassment when he traveled to Europe a few days later. Dozens of other lawyers and Internet activists were still held in detention without formal charges, while the harassment of others continued unabated. "I can't say if anything has changed," Pi San said, "but it was a big relief" to see Ai back in his home.

I dropped by Pi San's studio again in July. This time, I found his 7-year-old son, his head shaved for summer, sitting at his father's wooden desk and playing a game on an iPad. Pi San shuffled around in shorts and sandals, relaxed and happy. His wife, a fellow painter whom he met at college, worked on accounting ledgers at a table nearby.

Business had never been better. The first 10 episodes of "Ms. Puff" had pulled in an average of two million viewers, more than half of them women between 18 and 30. The Youku series's success raised ad rates, Hutoon's largest source of revenue, and several other Web portals had approached Pi San with offers, eager to entice his young viewers to their sites too.

In his darkest moments, Pi San vowed never to make another satire again. Shadowboxing with censors and security agents was too nerve-racking, and the risks to his family were too high. Now, in the wake of Ai's release, his fear was subsiding. "I think the government still looks at what I do as just cartoons, child's play," he said, struggling to explain why other artists and bloggers were detained or forced into exile while he escaped unscathed. It is a misconception Pi San is happy to embrace, even if, as he put it, "animated cartoons may be the most realistic way to capture the absurdity of our country."

Not long ago, Pi San started gravitating, once again, to the back room filled with miniature cardboard sets. "I think I have a few moves left," he said. He has already mapped out three new Kuang Kuang episodes. The theme of the next one? Pi San flashed a little grin. "It's a game of hide-and-seek."

BROOK LARMER lives in Beijing and writes for National Geographic and other publications.

Around the World in 80 Days for Cuba's Most Famous Dissident Blogger

BY LUISITA LOPEZ TORREGROSA | MARCH 5, 2013

WASHINGTON — Yoani Sanchez, Cuba's most famous dissident blogger, arrived in Brazil looking like a '60s hippie, her hair falling below her waist, her dark ankle-length skirt floating under a summery flower-child top. It was the first stop on Ms. Sanchez's 80-day tour of South America, Europe and the United States.

For the past few years, she's been a darling of both liberals and conservatives outside Cuba, a 37-year-old phenomenon, a fierce anti-Castro leader, a whip-smart intellectual and canny self-promoter. Her much awaited tour, her first trip outside Cuba in five years, comes with some of the fanfare reserved for major world figures.

I write the Cuban revolution's double-edged legacy when it comes to women's rights in my latest Female Factor column.

Ms. Sanchez, named by Time magazine one of the world's 100 most influential people in 2008 and a recipient of Columbia University's Maria Moors Cabot prize in 2009, is quite possibly the most famous living Cuban not named Castro.

The creator and instigator of the Generation Y blog — named after her first initial or after the Russian-influenced generation whose names start with a Y — Ms. Sanchez made a splashy landing in Brazil to the chants of fans and the shouts of opponents. Placards and banners accused her of complicity with the United States and betrayal of her country. Later, in Salvador, her second destination in Brazil, she had to evade demonstrators, but she seemed to enjoy the attention.

"At the arrival many friends were welcoming me and other people yelling insults. I wish it would be the same in Cuba. Long live freedom!" she exclaimed on Twitter.

Her elation needs little explanation. She has spent years risking her freedom at home while giving the world descriptions of the reality of daily life under the Castro regime. She has defied the authorities by sneaking her Generation Y blog out of Havana via stealth visits to Internet-equipped hotels where she manages to email her blogs to friends outside the country who then post them online. (The blog is said to be available in 17 languages.)

Now free, at least while she's abroad — and perhaps protected by her own fame — after defying authorities and facing arrest, beatings and kidnapping in Cuba, she's letting it all out with a vengeance.

Speaking about the protests against her in Brazil, she wrote: "I have experienced several acts of repudiation up close, whether as victim, observer, or journalist, never — I should clarify — as a victimizer. But last night was unprecedented for me. The picketing of the extremists...was something more than the sum of unconditional supporters of the Cuban government...They shouted, interrupted, and at one point became violent, and occasionally launched a chorus of slogans that even in Cuba are no longer said."

She went on, singing a hymn to herself, saying, "Their necks swelled, I cracked a smile. They attacked me personally; I brought the discussion back to Cuba which will always be more important than this humble servant. They wanted to lynch me; I talked. They were responding to orders; I am a free soul."

Within 24 hours of President Raul Castro's announcement on Feb. 24 that he would step down after his term ends in 2018 — and his subsequent designation of Miguel Diaz-Canel as first vice president and most likely successor — Ms. Sanchez was tearing up any illusions anyone could have about any loosening of the reins in Cuba.

"Diaz-Canel possesses characteristics that undoubtedly influenced his appointment," she wrote in her blog for The Huffington Post. "A man who shines very little, from whom we cannot recall a single phrase of his monotonous speeches, someone who projects absolute fidelity, a good physical presence and a dose of youth (52), so needed by Raul Castro to show that his government is generationally renewing itself." She cautioned that, given the fate of previous aspirants to the Castro seat, Mr. Diaz-Canel "awaits an uncertain journey fraught with booby-traps."

The journey Ms. Sanchez is on has its own perils. How free is she? What will happen when she returns to Cuba? Will she return? It's easy to see a scenario in which she settles in a European country, or even in the United States, living in freedom and surrounded by honors, comforts and money from speaking tours, blogs and books, and her family would probably be allowed to join her.

She married at age 18, in 1993, and had a son two years later. In 2002, she left Cuba and emigrated to Switzerland alone, but was later joined by her husband, Ricardo Escobar, and their son. They returned to the island in 2004, citing "family reasons."

She could pull up stakes again. But now it's different. Living as an exile, even a famous exile, she could lose the edge that sets her work apart. The mystery, what remains after so much publicity, would fade fast, and she would lose the aura of a prophet speaking truth in her own land.

Some of China's Prominent Internet Voices

BY CHRIS BUCKLEY | SEPT. 10, 2013

HONG KONG — Here are some popular people on Sina's Weibo and some of their recent messages.

Kai-Fu Lee is a Taiwanese high-tech investor who lives in Beijing and has more than 50 million followers. He attracted nationwide news media attention last week when he revealed on Weibo that he has lymphatic cancer. On Aug. 23, near the start of the crackdown on the most influential bloggers, or Big V's, Mr. Lee posted this: "Even faced with hardships and obstacles, I am full of confidence in China's social media, because I'm sure that China is now nurturing many friends with a sense of social responsibility, and they will give China a better future!"

尽管面临困难和障碍，我对中国社交媒体充满信心，因为我相信中国正在成长着为数众多的有社会责任感的朋友，他们将让中国的未来更好！

Yang Lan, a Chinese television celebrity with more than 34 million followers, usually sends messages about uncontroversial topics, including her interviews and philanthropic work. But recently, she has also criticized both restrictions on Internet expression and online attacks. She wrote on Aug. 23:

"Freedom of expression on the Internet, including voicing, debating and criticizing diverse points of view, is a force for social progress. But Internet rumors and freedom of expression are two different things, and we can all become victims of irrational linguistic violence. Whether it's protecting citizens' freedom of speech or protecting citizens' rights to their reputation and privacy, both should ultimately rest on rule of law."

网络上言论自由，包括多元观点的表达、争论、批评，是社会进步的推动力量。但网络谣言和言论自由是两回事，在非理性的语言暴力中，人人都可能成为受害者。无论保护公民言论自由，还是保护公民的名誉权、隐私权，最终还是要靠法治。希望尽快出台具体的司法解释。

Pan Shiyi, a property developer based in Beijing with more than 16 million followers, draws attention to the air pollution choking the city, and his messages played a significant role in forcing the government to take firmer action to reduce smog. Recently, he has also voiced misgivings about the government crackdown on Internet opinion. On Aug. 10, he posted this:

"Everyone is passionately discussing whether the Internet should be controlled, cleaned up, guided, to indoctrinate the public…I personally believe that everyone should participate in society online, and the public shouldn't be passively indoctrinated. Rumors should be sanctioned under the law. Forcing the Big V's and Internet celebrities to indoctrinate the public and raise the public's level of morality will not fly."

大家现在热烈讨论网络应该不应该管控、治理、引导、教化民众……。我个人认为：网络社会应该人人都参与，民众不应该是被动要教化、引导的对象。谣言应该受到法律制裁。让大V、网络名人去教化民众，提高民众的道德水平，这不靠谱。

Ye Haiyan, a businesswoman and feminist advocate with about 75,000 followers, promotes women's rights and urges stronger protection for sex workers. She wrote on Sept. 10:

"Looking at Weibo, there's an attitude of mutual crudeness between the public and the government — I'm rough on you, and you're rough on me — and an atmosphere of healthy communication hasn't formed. Those high up wave their big club back and forth to terrify people to death. The public's problem is that it demands that old and new problems are all tallied up, and gets worked up about small and big things. When will both sides calm down and have normal communication? I think those high up have to first give the weak a sense of security and respect."

从微博上看民间与政府的态度是互相粗暴，你对我粗暴，我对你粗暴，没有形成很好的沟通氛围。政府的问题是：高高在上，大棒子挥来挥去，吓死人。民间的问题是：新帐旧帐一起算，大事小事都反感。什么时候才能都双方冷静下来，正常沟通呢？我觉得还是高高在上的一方，要先让弱者有安全感，感觉被尊重。

Li Houlin, a Chinese jewelry businessman with 5.6 million followers, mixes his musings on society and commerce with criticisms of government policies. On Aug. 21, he criticized the crackdown on Internet rumors:

"These days when the spread of information has the capacity to have a real impact, each person must take responsibility for what he says. We must refuse rumors in the name of free speech, and must also avoid using the rhetoric about rumor to hinder freedom of speech. The most effective way to clean up rumors is not using state power to crack down, but letting the public promptly know the truth."

如今信息传递具有影响现实的能力，每个人都要对自己的言论负责任。既要杜绝打着言论自由旗号的谣言，也要避免拿谣言为说辞妨害言论自由。治理谣言最有效的办法不是公权打压，而是让民众第一时间知道真相。

The property developer **Ren Zhiqiang** has more than 15 million followers. He is one of the more outspoken voices on Weibo, using it to criticize government economic policy and take digs at rivals. Mr. Ren has also criticized government efforts to restrict comment. On Aug. 10 he wrote:

"If it weren't for Weibo, how much official corruption would be covered up? If it weren't for Weibo, how much rape and seduction by school presidents and principals would be covered up? If it weren't for Weibo, how much murder by city administration officers would be covered up? If it weren't for Weibo, how much of the truth would be covered up?"

如果没有微博会掩盖多少官员的贪腐？如果没有微博会掩盖多少院长与校长的奸淫？如果没有微博会掩盖多少城管的杀戮？如果没有微博会掩盖多少事实的真相？

Qandeel Baloch, Pakistani Social Media Celebrity, Dead in Apparent Honor Killing

BY SALMAN MASOOD | JULY 16, 2016

ISLAMABAD, PAKISTAN — Qandeel Baloch, a Pakistani social media sensation, was strangled by her brother in central Pakistan, police officials said Saturday, in what appears to have been a so-called honor killing.

The police said Ms. Baloch was apparently attacked on Friday night while she was asleep in her parents' house in Muzaffarabad, a town on the outskirts of Multan in the province of Punjab. Ms. Baloch's brother, Waseem Ahmed Azeem, was arrested late Saturday night in connection with her death.

Ms. Baloch, 26, a model, singer and social media celebrity, had gained notoriety in Pakistan recently because of provocative, seminude photographs of herself that she posted on social media sites, and appearances in music videos.

Her bold persona defied the conventions of Pakistan, a deeply conservative society. She was reviled by some in the country for being crass and vulgar, and prone to attention-seeking stunts. But other Pakistanis admired her defiance and independence. She attracted more than 700,000 followers on Facebook and at least 40,000 on Twitter.

"Qandeel was probably the first true female internet celebrity in Pakistan, in that her celebrity had nothing to do with any achievement beyond her provocative presence on social media," said Hasan Zaidi, a Pakistani filmmaker and media critic.

"It was unfathomable to a lot of Pakistanis that a real woman could be as brazen or shameless about her sexuality publicly, because her entire persona was built around flaunting her body, talking about sex and being in everyone's face," Mr. Zaidi said.

Ms. Baloch's latest appearance was in a video by an unknown singer, in which she danced provocatively to a song titled "Ban." The producers of the song anticipated that it could not be broadcast on mainstream entertainment channels and instead posted it on YouTube.

Born to a poor family from the backwaters of Punjab, Ms. Baloch, whose real name was Fauzia Azeem, said she had run away from home to pursue her dream of becoming a star. She took to social media after unsuccessful efforts to enter the mainstream entertainment industry.

In interviews, she acknowledged that she was pushing the traditional boundaries of socially acceptable behavior in Pakistan. "I know I exploited the freedom given to me by my parents," she said in an interview with BBC. "But now, it is too late."

In June, Ms. Baloch posted photographs of herself with a well-known Muslim cleric, Mufti Abdul Qavi, which attracted much attention on social media. The pictures show Ms. Baloch pouting and wearing the cleric's hat while he, seemingly bedazzled, stares into the camera.

Many Pakistanis saw the photographs as scandalous, and Mr. Qavi was removed from his position on the country's moon-sighting committee, which determines when Ramadan starts and ends in accordance with the Islamic lunar calendar.

On Wednesday, she found herself in the spotlight again after local media outlets reported that a man identified as her former husband claimed that he had a son with her and that he had divorced her after he could not meet her demands to provide a house and a luxury car. In response, Ms. Baloch said she had been a victim of domestic abuse.

Ms. Baloch was not shy about saying she wanted to be famous.

In a Twitter post on Wednesday, Ms. Baloch wrote: "I will fight for it. I will not give up. I will reach my goal & absolutely nothing will stop me."

The news of her death prompted an immediate outcry on Twitter and Facebook in Pakistan, with many people condemning her killing and praising Ms. Baloch for her irreverent and uninhibited ways.

"Qandeel Baloch was no role model," Sherry Rehman, an opposition politician and a former Pakistani ambassador to Washington, posted on Twitter. "But she deserved a better life and death. Strongly condemn."

The killing has put the spotlight back on so-called honor killings in Pakistan. Each year, hundreds of Pakistani women are killed by relatives angered by behavior they believe has tarnished the family's reputation, human-rights activists say.

Prime Minister Nawaz Sharif has vowed to strengthen laws intended to prevent such killings, but critics say no concrete steps have been taken yet.

In most cases, the honor killings take place within the family, said Syeda Sughra Imam, a former senator from Punjab who has pushed for legislation against the practice.

"The accused and the complainant are from the same family and they forgive each other," Ms Imam said. "No one is ever prosecuted."

Ms. Imam's proposed legislation calls for eliminating a "forgiveness clause" in Pakistani law that allows families to reach a financial settlement or to forgive the killer.

"This killing with impunity has to stop," Ms. Imam said.

ASIM TANVEER contributed reporting from Multan, Pakistan.

Chinese Censors Have New Target: Celebrity News

BY AMY QIN | JUNE 9, 2017

BEIJING — Whether read openly and voraciously or behind closed doors, celebrity gossip plays an integral role in the entertainment world, connecting stars and the big businesses that back them to an audience eager for the juiciest of details.

But to some officials in China, the bloggers that report those tidbits play another role: a threat to public order.

A large number of Chinese "celebrity news" blogs have disappeared in recent days after coming under the scrutiny of China's cyberspace regulators. Their absence comes amid a broader tightening of online and media controls ahead of a once-in-every-five-years meeting of top Communist Party leaders this year, at which party officials will consider major decisions about who will lead the country in the coming years.

At a meeting on Wednesday with representatives from China's leading internet companies, officials from the Beijing bureau of the Cyberspace Administration of China, the country's top online regulator, called on the companies to "actively promote socialist core values" and create a "healthy, uplifting environment for mainstream opinion" by combating vulgar and sensationalist coverage of celebrity scandals and lifestyles.

Since that meeting, reported by the state broadcaster China Central Television, major Chinese internet companies like Tencent and Baidu and the news aggregation platform Jinri Toutiao have shut down more than 80 popular entertainment-related public accounts, according to state news outlets. Many were on Tencent's WeChat social-media service, which is widely used in China and is increasingly a source of news and information.

Many of the closed blogs and accounts were making a tidy profit from advertising revenue, and some recently turned to venture capital investors as a route to growth. Zhuo Wei, known as China's No. 1 paparazzo, had more than seven million followers for his coverage of celebrities like the singer Faye Wong and the Chinese actress Bai Baihe. He could not immediately be reached for comment.

At least one of the closed accounts was affiliated with a global brand. The entertainment-related WeChat account of the fashion magazine Harper's Bazaar was shut down, although its account on Weibo, another social-media service, and its general WeChat account appeared to have survived. A spokesman for Harper's Bazaar could not immediately be reached for comment.

The closings prompted a swift outcry from China's media circles. While the local news industry has long been subjected to strict government censorship on politics and other topics deemed to be delicate, entertainment news has typically been viewed as safe.

"In China, there were only two areas before that we could say had news freedom: One was entertainment, and the other was sports," said Gao Ming, host of the podcast Radio HiLight and a former editor at AsiaContent.com, an online entertainment news company. "But now I think the government is trying to send a message that all the news needs to be within its control."

Using a Chinese phrase that means to make an example of someone or something, Mr. Gao added, "They're killing the chicken to scare the monkeys."

Of particular concern for many fans and industry watchers was the shutdown of popular entertainment-related accounts that were not in the business of trading celebrity gossip. One of these was the WeChat public account of the popular movie-review blog Dushe Dianying, which still had more than 4.8 million followers on Weibo. In July, the Chinese news media reported that Dushe Dianying was valued at about $44 million, after completing an early round of financing.

"Generally, China's leaders have been obsessed with the containment of negative coverage, and under Xi Jinping we've seen a rather dramatic decline in serious coverage by China's media," David

Bandurski, editor of the China Media Project at the University of Hong Kong, said in emailed comments, referring to the Chinese president. “What we’re now seeing is a war on the nonserious.”

“It’s no longer enough for media content to avoid the negative,” he added. “It must be adequately positive.”

The shutdowns come after a new cybersecurity law and new regulations issued by the Cyberspace Administration of China concerning the provision of news information through social media platforms like WeChat came into effect last week. According to the regulations, all online publishers — including websites, apps, blogs and social media accounts — must obtain permits from the authorities in order to publish news or news commentaries.

“These regulations could have quite a dramatic impact on the ecosystem of public accounts on WeChat, and on the broader online space,” Mr. Bandurski said. “This is something we must watch closely.”

Some of the affected accounts have already begun to regroup. By Thursday morning, Go Ying Studio, known for celebrity photographs and gossip, had created a new account and posted an official apology. “For us, this was a very profound lesson,” the statement read. “We wholeheartedly accept the criticism and help given to us by different corners of society, and from now on, we will make sure to strengthen our own thinking and moral education.”

But the future of many of the accounts remains uncertain — a cause for concern among the bloggers’ millions of fans.

“To me, it has become a habit to read some of these accounts every evening to relax,” lamented one reader, Luna, in a comment on a Chinese-language article about the deleted accounts. “People need these kinds of positive entertainment news. I am so sad.”

KAROLINE KAN contributed research.

Chinese Citizens Evade Internet Censors to Remember Liu Xiaobo

BY JAVIER C. HERNÁNDEZ | JULY 14, 2017

BEIJING — The death on Thursday of China's most prominent political prisoner, Liu Xiaobo, set off a frenzied effort by government censors to block discussion of his legacy online.

Candle emoticons and the phrase "R.I.P." were banned on Weibo, a popular Chinese microblogging site. On many sites, searches of Mr. Liu's name turned up zero results.

Still, Mr. Liu's admirers found creative ways around the controls, using code words, videos and photographs to show solidarity and to criticize the government's treatment of China's only Nobel Peace laureate.

'HEAVEN IS WATCHING'

When a thunderstorm erupted over Beijing shortly after Mr. Liu's death, internet users embraced the imagery.

"It must be to mark the exit of a hero," one Weibo user wrote. "The heavens are also moved."

"Heaven is watching," wrote a WeChat user, suggesting that China was being judged by a higher power for its treatment of Mr. Liu. The activist, who was awarded the Nobel Peace Prize in 2010, had been sentenced to 11 years for his efforts to promote democracy.

Activists have accused the government of depriving Mr. Liu of proper medical care after a cancer diagnosis. Some critics warned that the treatment of Mr. Liu has marred China's international reputation and tarnished the legacy of President Xi Jinping, who has taken a hard line against dissidents.

DENOUNCING CENSORSHIP

As censors sprung into action after Mr. Liu's death, internet users found creative means to convey their opinions. One popular motif was a picture of an empty chair, echoing the way the Nobel Prize committee honored Mr. Liu at the 2010 ceremony. Another common image was a black backdrop accompanied only by the text "1955-2017," the years of Mr. Liu's life.

Chinese journalists, lawyers and activists denounced government efforts to erase mentions of Mr. Liu. He is now relatively unknown in China, despite his fame overseas, and the mainland Chinese news media has largely not reported his death. To evade censors who were patrolling the internet for uses of Mr. Liu's name, some users instead referred to him as "Wang Xiaobo," or "Teacher Liu."

The censors were quick to react, blocking searches of several code words. A viral essay on Mr. Liu's death titled "A Night That Can't Be Discussed" was quickly deleted.

'NO ENEMIES'

Mr. Liu's famous phrase — "I have no enemies and no hatred" — was widely quoted among his admirers in the hours after his death. He had planned to make the remark at his sentencing on charges of inciting subversion of state power in 2009, but the court forbade him from doing so. Since then, the quotation has become a mantra of hope for pro-democracy activists in China and a reminder of Mr. Liu's commitment to nonviolence.

"I have no enemies and no hatred. None of the police who monitored, arrested and interrogated me, none of the prosecutors who indicted me, and none of the judges who judged me are my enemies," Mr. Liu wrote in a prepared statement in 2009.

As they grappled with his death, Mr. Liu's admirers quoted his writings and poetry. Some remembered his days helping student protesters gathered in Tiananmen Square in 1989. They posted photographs of a dimly lit square, a portrait of Mao blurry in the background.

"You are the martyr of freedom," wrote one user. "The executioner will never be forgiven."

IRIS ZHAO, **ZOE MOU** and **YE FEI** contributed research.

Know Your Chinese Social Media

BY YUAN REN | NOV. 19, 2018

SINA WEIBO

IF YOU WANT to go viral on social media or gain a mass audience in China, get on Weibo, China's Twitter and now the country's most popular microblogging site.

INTRODUCED August 2009, by the Chinese technology company Sina Corporation

USAGE 430 million active users a month (for comparison, Twitter has about 326 million)

CONTENT Official news channels have large followings, but there is little political content that is user-generated because censors quickly remove anything that is deemed sensitive. As a public platform, it's a launchpad of viral content and the place where online influencers, known as Key Opinion Leaders (K.O.L.s), go to amass a following — and perhaps turn their popularity into brand ambassador roles. Live streaming has become a crucial component of Weibo's offerings (the platform just acquired its live-streaming partner, Yizhibo) and is a major tool for K.O.L. engagement with their followers. In addition, Weibo Stories, which is similar to Instagram Stories, also allows users to upload short visual content.

A STAR Gogoboi, whose real name is Ye Si, has been called China's most famous fashion K.O.L. He was catapulted to fame when the actress Yao Chen — whose fan base of 80 million is one of the platform's largest — retweeted a post. Today, he has 9.3 million followers, and Gogoboi's one-hour backstage live stream of the Victoria's Secret show on Nov. 8 had been watched 2.5 million times by Nov. 12.

WECHAT

If you rolled all your phone apps into one, the result would be close to WeChat.

INTRODUCED January 2011 by Tencent, one of China's top tech companies

USAGE With one billion monthly active users, it is the most popular messaging app in China.

CONTENT Primarily a messenger app, WeChat can be used to do everything from hailing a cab to booking a hospital appointment — and payments can be made by WeChat Pay. But WeChat is a closed platform and account holders can see only what their friends post, which means brands can interact with subscribers on a personalized level. José Neves, founder of the e-tailer Farfetch, said at The New York Times International Luxury Conference last week in Hong Kong that, for a brand, "the first and foremost platform for your direct presence as a brand in China is WeChat." The platform's Mini Programs, third-party "apps" that run in WeChat without requiring downloads, increased to more than one million in 2018, used by brands such as Burberry, H&M, Dior and Longchamp.

A STAR Mr. Bags, the 26-year-old Tao Liang, has more than 4.6 million Weibo followers and 870,000 followers on his WeChat public account. He has collaborated with the likes of Montblanc and Givenchy and, in June, introduced a "BaoShop" Mini Program to sell a limited-edition bag created in collaboration with Tod's. The bag sold out within six minutes and generated 3.24 million renminbi, or $465,615, in sales.

JD

The two giants JD and Alibaba dominate e-commerce in China, with more than 80 percent of the market share.

INTRODUCED 1998

USAGE 314 million active monthly users

CONTENT JD operates the same business model as Amazon, acting as a direct retailer that controls the entire logistical chain of stock and distribution. Twenty percent of its investment comes from the tech giant Tencent, and it was the first e-commerce platform in China to bring same-day delivery to customers. On its website, it says that 90 percent of all purchases are delivered on the day of sale, or the next day.

Initially known for quality electronics and housewares, JD introduced its own luxury goods app, called Top Life, in October 2017. Its purchases are delivered by JD's Luxury Express service, a delivery man wearing a suit and white gloves.

A STAR The Swiss watch company Audemars Piguet is one of a host of brands, including Yves Saint Laurent and Alexander McQueen, that have signed onto the platform. (The watch company also is selling through its official WeChat store.)

ALIBABA

The e-commerce site grabbed headlines last week with news of its $30 billion in sales on Singles Day, the Nov. 11 shopping event it created 10 years ago.

INTRODUCED 1999

USAGE 552 million active users a month

CONTENT Unlike JD.com, Alibaba is an online marketplace for third-party retailers and has no inventory of its own. According to Wang Xiaofeng from Forrester, a market research company, Alibaba's stake in a host of businesses such as the food delivery app Ele.me allows it to aggregate a huge amount of data across different platforms and offer customized user recommendations. Alibaba's consumer-to-consumer platforms include Taobao, a vast virtual mall with more than 600 million active monthly users, known as the place to go for cheap and often counterfeit goods. (Many K.O.L.s have opened their own stores on Taobao and live-stream on the site to a majority female audience, half of whom are younger than 25.)

It also has Tmall, its business-to-consumer platform, which traditionally leans toward fashion and apparel, and Luxury Pavilion, an invitation-only portal for high-end goods introduced in August 2017.

A STAR Burberry, La Mer and Maserati are just some of the brands on the site.

DOUYIN, OR TIK TOK

Douyin (its international version is known as Tik Tok) is the younger, edgier "new kid" live-streaming site with shareable, snappy video content, as well as memes and GIFs to which users can add music, sound effects and emoticons.

INTRODUCED November 2017

USAGE 154 million active users a month

CONTENT Many of the K.O.L.s who were propelled into public view just a couple of years ago on live-streaming platforms like YY and Huajia are jumping ship to Douyin. The platform is popular with Generation Z, those younger than 24, but that youthful mass audience hasn't deterred fashion and luxury brands from creating official accounts. "The young are the ones who dare to spend in China," said Ms. Wang of Forrester, who attributes Douyin's success to a truly mobile-led era in which 79 percent of shoppers buy on their cellphone. "Douyin also has powerful machine learning capabilities, which means it continuously pushes content it knows the viewer will like, keeping them hooked."

A STAR Michael Kors was the first international label to debut on the platform. On the Chinese festival that is the equivalent of Valentine's Day, which was in August this year, Christian Dior introduced the Dioramour bag with five videos, including one from Angelababy, the K.O.L. who is a brand ambassador. In three months, and with 47 video posts, the channel now has more than 208,000 followers.

LITTLE RED BOOK, OR XIAOHONGSHU

The retail app, which began as a platform for review and discussion of products purchased abroad, says that trust is at the heart of what it promotes. It has become a social network for fashion and beauty products.

INTRODUCED 2014

USAGE 30 million active users a month

CONTENT A 2017 report by Bain showed that Chinese shoppers made three-quarters of their luxury purchases overseas, often through the diagou system, in which travelers and students buy luxury or hard-to-get items abroad and then sell them at a profit to people at home. (Diagou means "buy on behalf of.") Beijing recently has been trying to change the practice by easing import taxes, cracking down on travelers at customs entry points and supporting sales via large e-commerce platforms, as well as smaller sites like Little Red Book. The platform, which recently secured $300 million from investors including Alibaba, has A-list K.O.L.s, including Fan Bingbing, who debuted an account in January and, despite her recent tax problems, has more than 10 million fans. It has live-stream makeup tutorials and promotes her own Fanbeauty range, which can be purchased directly from Little Red Book.

A STAR The site really catapulted to popularity this year after it sponsored two of the country's most popular reality TV shows, including "Produce 101," a talent search for China's next big girl band.

FAST-GROWTH PLATFORMS

There are some growing names like Secoo, a luxury app that partnered with JD.com in August; Vipshop, which specializes in discounted goods and is the official "flash sales" platform of WeChat; Pinduoduo, a newcomer whose "group buy" model is popular with older shoppers seeking big discounts, and Mogujie, another shopping app popular with young women that has become WeChat's official women's style platform.

Learning China's Forbidden History, So They Can Censor It

BY LI YUAN | JAN. 2, 2019

Thousands of low-wage workers in "censorship factories" trawl the online world for forbidden content, where even a photo of an empty chair could cause big trouble.

LI CHENGZHI HAD a lot to learn when he first got a job as a professional censor.

Like many young people in China, the 24-year-old recent college graduate knew little about the 1989 Tiananmen Square crackdown. He had never heard of China's most famous dissident, Liu Xiaobo, the Nobel Peace Prize laureate who died in custody two years ago.

Now, after training, he knows what to look for — and what to block. He spends his hours scanning online content on behalf of Chinese media companies looking for anything that will provoke the government's wrath. He knows how to spot code words that obliquely refer to Chinese leaders and scandals, or the memes that touch on subjects the Chinese government doesn't want people to read about.

Mr. Li, who still has traces of youthful acne on his face, takes his job seriously. "It helps cleanse the online environment," he said.

For Chinese companies, staying on the safe side of government censors is a matter of life and death. Adding to the burden, the authorities demand that companies censor themselves, spurring them to hire thousands of people to police content.

That in turn has created a growing and lucrative new industry: censorship factories.

Mr. Li works for Beyondsoft, a Beijing-based tech services company that, among other businesses, takes on the censorship burden for other companies. He works in its office in the city of Chengdu. In the heart of a high-tech industrial area, the space is bright and new enough that it resembles the offices of well-funded start-ups in tech centers like

Beijing and Shenzhen. It recently moved to the space because customers complained that its previous office was too cramped to allow employees to do their best work.

"Missing one beat could cause a serious political mistake," said Yang Xiao, head of Beyondsoft's internet service business, including content reviewing. (Beyondsoft declined to disclose which Chinese media or online companies it works for, citing confidentiality.)

China has built the world's most extensive and sophisticated online censorship system. It grew even stronger under President Xi Jinping, who wants the internet to play a greater role in strengthening the Communist Party's hold on society. More content is considered sensitive. Punishments are getting more severe.

Once circumspect about its controls, China now preaches a vision of a government-supervised internet that has surprising resonance in other countries. Even traditional bastions of free expression like Western Europe and the United States are considering their own digital limits. Platforms like Facebook and YouTube have said that they would hire thousands more people to better keep a handle on their content.

Workers like Mr. Li show the extremes of that approach — one that controls what more than 800 million internet users in China see every day.

Beyondsoft employs over 4,000 workers like Mr. Li at its content reviewing factories. That is up from about 200 in 2016. They review and censor content day and night.

"We're the Foxconn in the data industry," said Mr. Yang, comparing his firm to the biggest contract manufacturer that makes iPhones and other products for Apple.

Many online media companies have their own internal content review teams, sometimes numbering in the thousands. They are exploring ways to get artificial intelligence to do the work. The head of the A.I. lab at a major online media company, who asked for anonymity because the subject is sensitive, said the company had 120 machine learning models.

JIALUN DENG

But success is spotty. Users can easily fool algorithms.

"The A.I. machines are intelligent, but they aren't as clever as human brains," Mr. Li said. "They miss a lot of things when reviewing content."

Beyondsoft has a team of 160 people in Chengdu working four shifts a day to review potentially politically sensitive content on a news aggregating app.

For the same app, Beyondsoft has another team in the western city of Xi'an reviewing potentially vulgar or profane content. Like the rest of the world, China's internet is rife with pornography and other material that many users might find offensive.

In the Chengdu office, workers must put their smartphones in hallway lockers. They can't take screenshots or send any information from their computers.

The workers are almost all college graduates in their 20s. They are often unaware of, or indifferent to, politics. In China, many parents and teachers tell the young that caring about politics leads only to trouble.

To overcome that, Mr. Yang and his colleagues developed a

sophisticated training system. New hires start with weeklong "theory" training, during which senior employees teach them the sensitive information that they didn't know before.

"My office is next to the big training room," Mr. Yang said. "I often hear the surprised sounds of 'Ah, ah, ah.' "

"They didn't know things like June 4," he added, referring to the 1989 Tiananmen Square crackdown. "They really didn't know."

Beyondsoft has developed an extensive database based on such information that Mr. Yang calls one of its "core competencies." It also uses anti-censorship software to regularly visit what it calls anti-revolutionary websites that are blocked by the Chinese government. It then updates the database.

New employees study the database much like preparing for college entrance exams. After two weeks, they have to pass a test.

The screen saver on each computer is the same: photos and names of current and past members of the Politburo Standing Committee, the Communist Party's top leadership. Workers must memorize those faces: Only government-owned websites and specially approved political blogs — a group on what's called a whitelist — are allowed to post photos of top leaders.

Workers are briefed at the beginning of their shift on the newest censoring instructions sent by clients, which the clients themselves receive from government censors. Workers then must answer about 10 questions designed to test their memory. The results of the exam affect the workers' pay.

One question on a recent Friday: Which one of the following names is the daughter of Li Peng, China's former premier? The correct answer is Li Xiaolin, a longtime target of online ridicule for her expensive fashion taste and for being one of many children of senior officials who come into high positions or wealth.

That's a relatively easy one. A tougher test is parsing the roundabout ways that China's internet users evade stringent censorship to talk about current affairs.

Take, for example, a Hong Kong news site's 2017 commentary that compared the six Chinese leaders since Mao Zedong to emperors during the Han dynasty. Some Chinese users started using the emperors' names when referring to the leaders. Beyondsoft's workers have to know which emperor's name is associated with which leader.

Then there are the photos of an empty chair. They refer to Mr. Liu, the Nobel laureate, who wasn't allowed to leave China to attend the award ceremony and was represented by an empty chair. References to George Orwell's novel "1984" are also forbidden.

Beyondsoft's software trawls through web pages and marks potentially offensive words in different colors. If a page is full of color-coded words, it usually requires a closer look, according to the executives. If there are only one or two, it's pretty safe to let it pass.

According to Beyondsoft's website, its content monitoring service, called Rainbow Shield, has compiled over 100,000 basic sensitive words and over three million derivative words. Politically sensitive words make up one-third of the total, followed by words related to pornography, prostitution, gambling and knives.

Workers like Mr. Li make $350 to $500 a month, about average pay in Chengdu. Each worker is expected to review 1,000 to 2,000 articles during a shift. Articles uploaded to the news app must be approved or rejected within an hour. Unlike Foxconn workers, they don't work much overtime because longer hours could hurt accuracy, said Mr. Yang, the executive.

It's easy to make mistakes. One article about Peng Liyuan, China's first lady, mistakenly used the photo of a famous singer rumored to be linked to another leader. It was caught by someone else before it went out, Mr. Yang said.

Mr. Li, the young censor, said the worst mistakes were almost all related to senior leaders. He once missed a tiny photo of Mr. Xi on a website not on the whitelist because he was tired. He still kicks himself for it.

When asked whether he had shared with family and friends what he learned at work, such as the Tiananmen crackdown, Mr. Li vehemently said no.

"This information is not for people outside to know," he said. "Once many people know about it, it could generate rumors."

But the crackdown was history. It wasn't a rumor. How would he reconcile that?

"For certain things," he said, "one just has to obey the rules."

PewDiePie Put in Spotlight After New Zealand Shooting

BY NIRAJ CHOKSHI | MARCH 15, 2019

ONE OF YOUTUBE'S biggest celebrities found himself entangled early Friday in news coverage of the mass shooting at two mosques in New Zealand.

A gunman who had broadcast part of the attack that left at least 49 people dead urged those watching to "subscribe to PewDiePie," referring to the alias used by Felix Kjellberg, a Swede whose channel has long dominated YouTube and courted controversy along the way.

Mr. Kjellberg was quick to distance himself from the shooting.

"I feel absolutely sickened having my name uttered by this person," he said on Twitter. "My heart and thoughts go out to the victims, families and everyone affected by this tragedy."

Mr. Kjellberg is no stranger to controversy. In recent years, he has been embraced by some on the far right and faced criticism for his use of anti-Semitic imagery and racist and sexist language. Here is a closer look at PewDiePie and the New Zealand gunman's words.

WHO IS PEWDIEPIE?

As PewDiePie, Mr. Kjellberg has amassed a following of 89 million YouTube subscribers over the past decade with videos that feature a mix of comedic rants, commentary and video game narration.

Though edited, the videos carry an intimate, unguarded aesthetic that has helped Mr. Kjellberg remain relevant and sought after by advertisers. According to Forbes, a sponsored video with PewDiePie can cost up to $450,000. Mr. Kjellberg earned $15.5 million last year.

THE MEANING OF 'SUBSCRIBE TO PEWDIEPIE'

There's more to the gunman's words — "subscribe to PewDiePie" — than meets the eye.

Kevin Roose, a columnist for The New York Times, wrote on Friday that the message may have served two purposes: to inflame political tensions and to serve as a knowing nod to those who might be watching the gunman's actions with approval.

To achieve those ends, the gunman, who has not been officially identified, used a meme born out of a competition for YouTube dominance.

Last year, T-Series, a music label and film production company based in India, emerged as a threat to PewDiePie's top-ranked status on YouTube.

In response, Mr. Kjellberg jokingly rallied his fans to stave off T-Series, even going so far as to make a comedic diss track to play up the competition. Other YouTubers got in on the fight, too, with some buying radio and display advertising.

As with many other oft-repeated phrases online, "subscribe to PewDiePie" became a symbol, a meme, unto itself.

EMBRACED BY THE FAR RIGHT

In 2017, Disney severed ties with Mr. Kjellberg and YouTube distanced itself from him after The Wall Street Journal identified at least nine of his videos that featured anti-Semitic gestures and imagery.

In one, a pair of men hired by Mr. Kjellberg unfurled a sign that read "Death to All Jews" and then laughed and danced. In another, he wears a brown military uniform, nodding along to archival footage of Hitler delivering a speech.

Some of the videos were removed and Mr. Kjellberg described the segments as jokes, saying in a statement that he was "in no way supporting any kind of hateful attitudes" and that "I understand that these jokes were ultimately offensive."

Despite those comments, members of the far-right embraced what Mr. Kjellberg had done.

A post on The Daily Stormer, a neo-Nazi website, noted that the videos raised questions about Mr. Kjellberg's own views, but concluded that they didn't matter: "The effect is the same; it normalizes Nazism, and marginalizes our enemies."

In an article last year, Paul MacInnes, who writes on sports and popular culture for The Guardian, faulted mainstream publications for largely ignoring Mr. Kjellberg.

"To call him an alt-right agitator would perhaps be unfair as he has never publicly identified with the proto-fascist movement," Mr. MacInnes wrote. "But he shares much of their culture and amplifies it across the world. People should pay PewDiePie more attention."

OTHER CONTROVERSIES

Later in 2017, Mr. Kjellberg used a racial slur during a video game live-stream, which he later described as "extremely immature and stupid."

"I said the worst word I could possibly think of, and it just sort of slipped out and I'm not going to make any excuse as to why," he said in a video apologizing for his use of the word.

Last year, Mr. Kjellberg got into a feud with Natalia Mogollon, another online personality famous on Twitch, where she goes by the alias Alinity Divine and narrates live-streams of video games.

In a video testing out an eye-tracking device, Mr. Kjellberg jokingly referred to women in one of the videos he watched, including Ms. Mogollon, as "stupid Twitch thots," a derogatory term.

Ms. Mogollon took offense. In an ensuing back-and-forth, Mr. Kjellberg suggested that she intentionally dresses provocatively on her stream.

"Oh, you're just playing games with the shortest skirt ever, that's our fault for looking at it in any sexual way, right?" he said.

A few months later, he was criticized as insensitive for sharing a meme that made light of the singer Demi Lovato's struggle with drugs.

CHAPTER 5

A Dangerous Place

Wherever lots of people congregate — in person or online — bad behavior is bound to rear its ugly head. Cyberbullying combines online harassment with other acts of aggression to insult and harm others. Influencers are not immune to such acts. A number of celebrities have suffered at the hands of such bullies themselves. The famous can also be the target of hackers who seek to blackmail them with the threat of sharing personal data. Some influencers depend on ad revenue from their online efforts, and the loss of that can send them over the edge and lead to violence.

For $1,000, Site Lets Celebrities Say It Ain't So

BY SARAH LYALL | MARCH 27, 2011

LONDON — Imagine you are a well-known person aggrieved by how you are portrayed on the Internet: the slapdash Wikipedia entry; the unflattering gossip item; the endlessly repeated story about how you cheated on your spouse when in point of fact you were blamelessly resuscitating a platonic friend who was choking on an olive.

Suing is too stressful and quixotic. Besides, it's the Internet: how can anyone erase the inerasable? But courtesy of a new Web site called ICorrect, people who feel unhappy about "obvious misinterpretations, misinformation and what some might call total lies," in the words of the site's founder, Sir David Tang, can now attempt to set the record straight.

"The superhighway is jampacked with stops where at every place you'll have mud thrown at you," said Sir David, 56, a businessman, socialite and celebrity friend extraordinaire who is best known for founding the department store chain Shanghai Tang. "Can you afford to have it all stick and not try to clean it up?"

People concerned about their reputations can use the site to post as many corrections as they want, for $1,000 a year. Luckily, browsing through the posts is free.

Here is the actor Stephen Fry, rebutting a report that he dislikes Catholics. Here is the businessman Richard Caring, noting that he did not rudely fail to turn up at an important luncheon (it was a misunderstanding).

Meanwhile, Cherie Blair, wife of former Prime Minister Tony Blair, did not appear at a party wearing the same dress as the actress Hayden Panettiere; did not go shooting with Col. Muammar el-Qaddafi's son; and never declared that a burqa "is no more a threat than a nun's habit."

Sienna Miller would like to make it clear that she is not on Twitter. Tommy Hilfiger never said that he did not want black people to wear his clothes. And, despite what you may have heard, Viscount and Viscountess Linley were not sulking in a maritally discordant way after a recent wedding (they were, the viscount writes, "just waiting for our car").

ICorrect went live this month and has about 35 founding members, or correctors, as they are called, plucked mostly from the pages of Sir David's very thick book of contacts. Anyone can join, with payment and proof that he is who he claims to be; the site does not post items from nonmembers.

Sir David said that the site, apparently helped by a positive Twitter message from Mr. Fry, had 225,000 hits its first weekend. "It's minimally designed to make sure that even the most stupid person can work it and understand it," he said.

Although Sir David admits that it has been "quite a path to persuade people to join," he has high hopes that someday ICorrect will be the world clearinghouse for corrections. "It's my fervent desire to have NGO's and big corporations like BP," he said.

The new venture has been greeted with some skepticism in the British media world, in part because some people thought at first that it was a joke, and in part because many journalistic commentators are not naturally sympathetic to offended celebrities.

"As images of human desolation were beamed into our homes this week," wrote Brian Reade in the Daily Mirror tabloid, referring to the Japanese tsunami, "rich and famous people were hunched over laptops alerting us to the grotesque injuries caused to their reputations."

Stephen Pritchard, the ombudsman at The Observer of London, which has an actual corrections column, said in an interview that people who joined ICorrect risked drawing unnecessary attention to the very items they wished would go away. Also, he added, who is to say whether their corrections are in fact themselves correct, rather than fake alternatives they wish were true?

That is not the point. "We're not here to police it or prove the veracity of what you post," Sir David explained, "although we do make sure you don't commit crimes by defaming people or inciting others to violence."

The beauty of the site, he said, is that it allows the offending items to be viewed next to the offended person's response, so that even lazy Internet users will be exposed to both sides of any given story.

"A lot of people simply look up Google and press a finger and lift whatever is in front of them," Sir David said.

For example, he added, "If you say that Henry Kissinger bombed Cambodia illegally, you will have to do a bit of research before you find where he defends himself. But if he joins the site, he can say, 'This was my reason, and it's more fully explained on pages 85 and 86 of my autobiography.' "

Meanwhile, Mrs. Blair, who became a popular target for tabloid tales when her husband was prime minister, said that in a country where some newspapers made little effort to "get the basic facts of a story right," the site was a welcome antidote.

ANDREW TESTA FOR THE NEW YORK TIMES

Sir David Tang, founder of the iCorrect Web site, at his home in London on Thursday.

"Anything which allows people publicly to correct factual inaccuracies in stories about them is a good idea," she said in an e-mail message.

Of course. But on the other hand, one of ICorrect's members is Bianca Jagger, and all you can do in reading her entries is sit back in dismay as the myths fall.

No, Ms. Jagger says, she did not go out with Pierre Trudeau, the former prime minister of Canada. No, Billy Joel's song "Big Shot," about a woman riding in a limousine with "the Dom Perignon in your hand and the spoon up your nose," is not based on a bad date he had with her.

She also addresses the business about herself, the horse and Studio 54, revealing that, unfortunately, it was not as exciting as everyone thought.

As one visitor to the site, Laura LaRue, said on Twitter: "ICorrect is making me a little sad. Bianca Jagger did not ride a white horse half-naked in Studio 54. Sometimes a lie is more fun?"

On Facebook, Bullies 'Like' if You Hate

BY EMILY LAYDEN | SEPT. 9, 2012

FOR THE DIGITALLY native generation, self-worth is accrued in likes.

My little brother went to school on a Friday morning last June, and this is what he heard: That another boy, a sixth-grader, had written a Facebook status the previous night asking his friends to "like" it if they hated my brother. The "like if you hate" question, the last time this informant had checked, had gotten 57 thumbs-up. Verification for my brother's generation — the younger half of my own — is a statistical rat race, counted in friends, followers, re-tweets and re-pins. On an ordinary Friday morning, my brother learned that his name had garnered 57 "like if you hates."

This is a hard thing for me to imagine: 57 likes for a hate — a hate for a person, a little boy, my little brother. But it's more macroscopic, too. There is a marked difference between how my half-generation and my brother's engages with and approaches the Internet. I remember dial-up and still have my AOL.com e-mail address (it's basically a giant spam folder, now). I weed through my Facebook friends weekly, de-friending those whose names I don't remember or maybe never really knew. I have friends with separate work and personal Twitter accounts and those who take weekends off from the Web. We deal with the Internet with separation. It is a tool to be used and put away.

For my brother's half — the younger set, the one that did not grow up in step with the Internet, but rather with it already established — there is no wariness, no understanding, no concept of an Internet identity. There is no such thing for them, for example, as "Internet famous." There is only fame, and the allure of instant gratification. This is how cyberbullying has reached a fever pitch, and where I feel my half of this generation has failed the younger.

We (my peers) use the numbers game. We understand how to turn hits on Web sites into ad sales, how to drive traffic, how to analyze page views and visitors for a better understanding of successful content — this is a legitimate business practice. We have done an abysmal job of translating this understanding to the younger half. Instead, we have allowed an entire half-generation to believe, simply, that more is more: To measure their existence against how many thousands of friends they have, how many hundreds more they have than their classmates, how many likes they can get.

This fact alone is toxic enough, but far worse is that we have taught them the secret to a quick hit, a fast follow: a cheap shot. Web sites like BuzzFeed and Gawker (and its sister sites Deadspin and Jezebel) operate with a vicious reliance on views, so that any press is good press. Rage-baiting is commonplace and infuriatingly successful, so the most prevalent language of the Internet is at its best cynicism and its worst outright meanness. (This is all, of course, made worse by the hammered-home fact that it is so easy to be cruel behind the safety of a computer screen. The cowardice is obvious.)

So my half of the generation (those of us in our 20s, the ones with job titles like "social media manager," the developers of apps like Instagram and Path), in not communicating the difference between work and Web, between the Internet and reality, has allowed the younger set to seek personal validation in Internet numbers. We have shown them that the easiest way to do so is through varying degrees of cruelty. To eliminate cyberbullying, we must better address the Internet-bred narcissism at its core, and we must all be held accountable. Both the older set of digital natives and the generation above us assume that the Internet is a bubble — a space with limits. This is the logic behind the cyberbullying stance at my brother's school, who informed my parents in the wake of the 57 likes that cyber bullying is a "tricky" matter that unfortunately falls largely outside their jurisdiction.

There is no jurisdiction for the bullied, no separation between Web and reality. On the Monday after the Facebook incident, my brother dreaded school for fear of facing his 57 bullies, who probably never gave their likes a second thought. The answer is not to teach our middle-schoolers that they are not who they are online. It is, actually, quite the opposite. It is too late to establish distance. To end cyberbullying, we must use the closeness we've allowed to breed to our advantage. We must teach them that if one is a cowardly, bullying, rage-baiter online — no matter how many laughs had or page views generated or ad space sold — then one is a bully off-screen, too.

The Latest Celebrity Diet? Cyberbullying

CRITIC'S NOTEBOOK | BY AMANDA HESS | OCT. 12, 2016

THE REALITY TV STAR Rob Kardashian had a family matter to discuss, so naturally, he turned to Twitter. "Didn't invite the Mother of my child to a baby shower you all were trying to throw for me!!?" he tweeted late last month, reigniting the feud between the Kardashian-Jenner clan and his model fiancée, Blac Chyna. "You all must have lost your damn minds." In retaliation for the slight, he tweeted out his little sister Kylie Jenner's phone number.

Mr. Kardashian, in internet parlance, had doxxed Ms. Jenner — he published personal, private information about her online, seemingly without her consent. It's a maneuver harassers use to humiliate, intimidate or silence their targets. It also helped Mr. Kardashian score his most popular tweet ever.

Lately, celebrity feuds have taken on the contours of cyberbullying, with famous rivals integrating the tactics of online harassers into their P.R. offensives. What looks like a public display of immaturity can actually be part of a sophisticated image management strategy. Retweet counts and Instagram followers are the new Billboard 100, and celebrities can gin up their numbers by instigating feuds with one another in increasingly nasty or technologically intriguing ways. But the game can have a dark side, especially for the losers.

The modern celebrity arsenal incorporates these other digital bullying tools:

SECRET RECORDINGS The celebrity squabble of the summer exploded when Kim Kardashian West released a surreptitiously recorded Taylor Swift talking on the phone with Ms. Kardashian West's husband, Kanye West — a bid to prove that Ms. Swift had preapproved his controversial lyrics about her in his song "Famous." Ms. Kardashian West posted the video evidence to Snapchat in July. (Such recordings are illegal in some states, including California, and run afoul of YouTube's harassment rules.)

SEXUAL HUMILIATION When the rappers Wiz Khalifa and Mr. West tussled on Twitter in January, Amber Rose, their mutual ex, stepped in to tease Mr. West about their sex life. And when Justin Bieber's ex-girlfriend Selena Gomez waded into his Instagram comments to scold him for posting pictures with a new girlfriend and to accuse him of cheating on her, he struck back by accusing her of using the relationship for attention.

REVENGE PORN After the teenage actress Chloë Grace Moretz tweeted dismissively about the Kardashian-Swift feud, yet another Kardashian — Kim's sister Khloé — responded by posting a photo of a woman resembling Ms. Moretz. She had jumped onto a young man's back on the beach, and her bikini bottoms were yanked to the side, revealing everything underneath. Ms. Moretz tweeted back to debunk the depantsing, writing that Ms. Kardashian had instead exposed "some girl who was wrongfully photographed."

MOB DEPLOYMENT For celebrities with the most rabid fandoms, even an oblique nod from the star can set off a fan stampede. After Ms. Kardashian West posted the Snapchat video of Ms. Swift's phone call, Kanye fans and allies — many aligned with her spurned ex-boyfriend Calvin Harris — gathered under the #KimExposedTaylorParty hashtag to shovel out cruelly exultant GIFs and memes. (A commemorative T-shirt reading "In Memory of Taylor Swift, RIP, 1989 to 2016" was soon offered for sale online.) And when Ms. Kardashian West cryptically tweeted a line of snake emoji, revelers bombarded Ms. Swift's Instagram with snake after snake after snake.

It's no coincidence that a Kardashian fingerprint can be lifted from many of the most high-profile incidents. While most celebrities use the internet to promote their mainstream careers — movies, albums — Ms. Kardashian West's core product is herself. Stirring up dramatic personal narratives on her reality television show and social media accounts is her main event. Ms. Swift, who studiously avoids confrontation while writing veiled riddles about her ex-boyfriends and frenemies into her songs, didn't stand a chance.

And she went on to milk the publicity by posting another Snapchat video of herself singing along to the "Famous" lyrics in question. Her clip became an internet blockbuster not only because of the story it told but also because of the tactics it deployed. In the polished world of celebrity P.R., it's exceptional to see a celebrity exposed in a private moment, especially by one of her own kind. Meanwhile, Ms. Swift was put on the defensive, left to quibble about the details of the exchange in a long-winded message that she typed on Apple's Notes app. She then took a screen shot of it and posted it to Instagram. Her self-serious response to Ms. Kardashian West's raucous exposé — "I would very much like to be excluded from this narrative" — soon curdled into a mocking meme. Who was in the right didn't matter — Ms. Kardashian West won the game.

Blac Chyna, who recently clawed her way into the Kardashian universe through her relationship with Rob, has proved a quick study. A few days after Mr. Kardashian doxxed his sister, Ms. Chyna posted his number to Twitter, too, then toggled over to Snapchat to explain that she'd done it to compel her fiancé to change his number — and flush out all the women who had been texting him. It was a strategic move, both personally and professionally — it locked down her man, drew attention to her suite of social accounts and stirred interest in the couple's E! reality series, "Rob & Chyna."

You'd think that the utter savageness on display here would horrify fans. Online celebrity feuds capitalize on some of the most vile and destructive social ideas: that sexual shaming is an acceptable response to a stated opinion; that women are manipulative liars; and that a person who missteps in a private dispute deserves to be punished by the crowd. And these days, nearly everybody has a story about being subjected to similar abuse online.

Occasionally, celeb-on-celeb attacks backfire: In May, the rapper Azealia Banks posted a racist tirade against the pop star Zayn Malik and soon found herself booted from Twitter for violating its harassment policy. But most of the time, salty celebrities have little to lose and millions of followers to gain. “Bullying” and “harassment” are amorphous categories, and the seriousness we attach to these tactics varies considerably depending on the power dynamics at play. Unlike the muscled jock who picks on the scrawny nerd, the straight teenager who harasses the gay kid or the jilted boyfriend who uses the cover of the internet to mar his ex’s reputation, these celebrity cases can make us feel like mere mortals peering up at a couple of Greek gods shooting lightning bolts at each other. For some fans, their own experiences with harassment may fuel their desire to see the rich and famous get dragged down to their level. Instead of pity and concern for the targeted party, celebrity harassment produces in fans feelings of both fascination and schadenfreude.

For the famous person caught in the cross hairs, though, it’s not always so fun. Just ask Ms. Swift, who called Ms. Kardashian West’s stunt “character assassination.” Or the pop star Demi Lovato, who announced a career hiatus last week after getting dragged across Twitter over dismissive comments about Ms. Swift she made in a magazine interview. (“Taking a break from the spotlight,” Ms. Lovato tweeted last week. “I am not meant for this business and the media.”) Or Ms. Moretz, who did not deserve to be sexually humiliated for subtweeting Ms. Kardashian West.

It’s a P.R. game, until it’s a real thing.

Man Who Hacked Celebrities' Email Accounts Gets 5 Years in Prison

BY BENJAMIN WEISER | DEC. 6, 2016

A BAHAMIAN MAN who hacked into the email accounts of celebrities and athletes and later wrote in a jailhouse email that after his release he would "shake up hollywood for real!" was sentenced to five years in prison on Tuesday.

The sentence was roughly double the number of years suggested under federal sentencing guidelines.

The man, Alonzo Knowles, 24, had used his illicit access to the celebrity accounts to obtain unreleased movie and television scripts and personal information, which he then tried to sell for thousands of dollars, prosecutors said. Mr. Knowles had also stolen unreleased music, financial documents, and nude and intimate images and videos, the government said.

Kristy J. Greenberg, a prosecutor, said in Federal District Court in Manhattan that Mr. Knowles's motivation had been greed. "He had a singular focus on becoming rich and famous," she said, "by disseminating personal information of celebrities and exploiting them."

Several victims had submitted statements to the judge. Naturi Naughton, an actress in the Starz drama "Power," said in a video statement that Mr. Knowles had hacked her personal emails and stolen six scripts of the show, and then "tried to extort me, the producer, 50 Cent and my showrunner."

"I have never felt more violated and out of control in my entire life," Ms. Naughton said.

Judge Paul A. Engelmayer of Federal District Court called Mr. Knowles's crimes "deeply troubling," and told him that he had chosen to use "your gifts, your know-how, for dark and lawless ends."

When Mr. Knowles pleaded guilty in federal court in May, he apologized, saying he knew what he had done was wrong. But he then wrote in emails sent from jail that he planned to write a book and reveal the secrets of the victims whose accounts he had broken into, the government said.

"Im name dropping everyone involved and what I know," Mr. Knowles wrote, "and im including pictures of paperwork that aint public."

He wrote that he would charge $35 a copy, would hack into Twitter accounts to promote his book and that his goal was to make money. "Everyone loves gossip," he wrote. "I cant wait to get out i already know how the cover is gonna look."

The emails, which prosecutors cited in a sentencing memorandum to Judge Engelmayer, had been sent on a Bureau of Prisons email system that prisoners may use after they give consent to the monitoring of their messages.

The judge said that Mr. Knowles's jailhouse messages were "devoid of any remorse," and showed that if he were released from prison any time soon, he "would be a clear and present danger to commit the very same crime again."

"Unavoidably, Mr. Knowles," Judge Engelmayer said, "the public has a significant interest in your being behind bars in federal prison where you have no access to the internet and no practical ability to do such harm."

Mr. Knowles, who had pleaded guilty to charges of identity theft and criminal copyright infringement, read a brief statement, apologizing to the court and his victims. "What I did was wrong," he said. "I could have ruined people's lives."

His lawyer, Clay Kaminsky, had asked for a sentence of 14 months. Mr. Knowles had faced a maximum sentence of 10 years; the federal sentencing guidelines, which are not binding on a judge, had suggested 27 to 33 months, his plea agreement shows.

Mr. Knowles was arrested last December after he flew to New York to meet with a man who was posing as a potential buyer of the scripts he had stolen. The man was actually an undercover agent.

The case drew attention in part because it followed the widely publicized hacking of Sony Pictures Entertainment in 2014. The Knowles case also showed how a hacker could obtain confidential information from victims by targeting the accounts of their friends and associates, a process Mr. Knowles called “social engineering.”

“In the wee hours of the night, when his victims were likely asleep, Knowles trolled his victims’ private email accounts, obtaining their most personal communications,” the office of Preet Bharara, the United States attorney for the Southern District of New York, had said in its sentencing memorandum.

Sleeping in Car and Visiting Gun Range: How YouTube Attacker Spent Final Hours

BY DAISUKE WAKABAYASHI, MATTHEW HAAG AND ELIZABETH DIAS | APRIL 4, 2018

• INVESTIGATORS ON WEDNESDAY said they believed YouTube's policies had motivated a woman to shoot three people at the company's headquarters in San Bruno, Calif., before killing herself.

• The attacker, identified as Nasim Najafi Aghdam, had been seen at a nearby shooting range before the attack, and a gun registered in her name was found at the scene.

• Ms. Aghdam, who was in her late 30s and had lived in Southern California, often discussed Persian culture, veganism and animal cruelty; performed music parodies; and gave exercise tutorials on YouTube and on her personal website.

HOW THE ATTACKER SPENT HER LAST DAY

The police in Mountain View, Calif., about 30 miles south of San Bruno, said they had found Ms. Aghdam sleeping in a car near a shopping center around 1:40 a.m. on Tuesday. The car was parked a few miles from the headquarters of Google, YouTube's parent company.

The officers soon discovered that the vehicle was connected to a person who had been reported missing on March 31 in San Diego County, the Mountain View police said on Wednesday.

Ms. Aghdam told Mountain View officers that she was not a danger to herself or to others and that she had traveled to the San Francisco area to look for a job, the police said. She was interviewed for about 20 minutes, the police said.

"At no point during our roughly 20-minute interaction with her did she mention anything about YouTube, if she was upset with them, or that she had planned to harm herself or others," the Mountain View police said in a statement posted on the department's website. "Throughout our entire interaction with her, she was calm and cooperative."

After the conversation ended, the officers called Ms. Aghdam's family to say she had been located, the police said. The family did not mention anything about YouTube at the time, the police said. But her father and brother called back about an hour later and told the police she had made a series of videos about veganism that she had posted on YouTube.

"At no point did her father or brother mention anything about potential acts of violence or a possibility of Aghdam lashing out as a result of her issues with her videos," the police said in the statement.

Chief Barberini declined to comment on local reports that Ms. Aghdam's family had warned the police in Mountain View that she was headed toward YouTube's offices. But he said that it received no information in advance of the shooting.

HANDGUN WAS REGISTERED TO AGHDAM

During the attack, Ms. Aghdam fired "multiple shots" from a Smith & Wesson 9-millimeter, semiautomatic handgun, Ed Barberini, chief of the San Bruno police department, said on Wednesday. The gun, which was registered to her, was recovered at the scene.

There is no evidence linking Ms. Aghdam to any of the shooting victims, Chief Barberini said. Investigators were searching two homes in Southern California associated with the suspect.

On Tuesday morning, before driving to the YouTube offices, Ms. Aghdam visited a local gun range, the police said.

Ms. Aghdam parked her car at a business near YouTube. She entered one of the company's parking garages, and then walked into an outdoor courtyard where employees were eating lunch. The chief said that investigators were still trying to determine what level of security there was in the area leading to the courtyard. Zach Vorhies, a YouTube engineer, said on Tuesday that the dining area was accessible from an adjacent parking structure without an employee badge.

"At this point in the investigation, it is believed that the suspect was upset at the policies and practices of YouTube. This appears to be the motive for this incident," Mr. Barberini said.

The chief said his department had worked with YouTube to develop security measures for the campus, including what to do in the case of an armed attacker.

The three shooting victims were taken to Zuckerberg San Francisco General Hospital. Two women, a 32-year-old who was admitted in serious condition and a 27-year-old who was admitted in fair condition, were released late on Tuesday, a hospital spokesman said.

The third shooting victim, a 36-year-old man, had improved from critical to serious condition and remained in the hospital.

YOUTUBE EMPLOYEES BRIEFLY VISIT OFFICE

On Wednesday morning, the area around YouTube's office in San Bruno, a suburban community of 41,000 people that stretches into the hills above Silicon Valley, was quiet. Police officers, security guards, news reporters and a handful of employees milled around outside the building.

Police had cordoned off the street in front of the offices, but company security guards were allowing small groups of employees into the building from a lower-level entrance.

A few workers in hard hats and florescent yellow vests from a company called Restoration Management Company — a firm that specializes in services cleaning up "trauma scenes," according to its website — carried plastic bags of debris out of the building.

Like many communities on the peninsula stretching south from San Francisco to San Jose, San Bruno is a mix of office parks and single-family homes. The last time the city received national attention was in 2010, when a natural gas explosion killed eight people and destroyed a neighborhood.

YouTube employees on Wednesday appeared to spend no more than 10 minutes inside before exiting the building. A few employees, who asked not to be identified because they had been told not to speak to the news media, said they were picking up items left behind after they fled the building during the attack. Some said they were there to pick up their cars — a few people drove vehicles out of a closed parking garage that police said Ms. Aghdam used to enter the YouTube facility on Tuesday.

But in other buildings in the YouTube complex, it appeared to be a regular work day. At a YouTube office across the street from the main headquarters, employees ate lunch in a fenced off courtyard.

A SOCIAL MEDIA STAR IN IRAN

In Iran, Ms. Aghdam was known as "Green Nasim," a social media star with followings on YouTube, on Instagram and elsewhere who was sometimes admired and sometimes mocked.

Ms. Aghdam had YouTube pages in Persian, Turkish and English. In several of her videos she stated that she had been born in Iran, in the city of Urmia, near the border with Turkey. She explained in videos that she and her family are members of the Baha'i faith, a persecuted minority in majority Muslim Iran.

It was perhaps her inability to easily fit a stereotype that drew her to so many in Iran, where she had tens of thousands of followers on social media. Several of her colorful — and sometimes bizarre — videos had gone viral.

Life in the United States had not been good, she said in one video posted last week. "There they kill you by ax," she said of Iran. "Here they kill you with cotton" — an Iranian expression meaning to die by something that you do not know is dangerous.

In another video, she responded to viewers who had begun to wonder if she was mentally ill: "I don't have any special mental or physical disease, but I live on a planet filled with disease, disorders, perversions and injustices."

HUNT FOR CLUES MOVES QUICKLY ONLINE

Ms. Aghdam had told her family in recent weeks that she "hated" YouTube because it was censoring her videos and paying her less. "She was angry," her father, Ismail Aghdam, who lives outside Los Angeles in Riverside County, told the Bay Area News Group.

"When searching for my website in google, at top of link they add 'an error occurred' but there is no error!" a website under her name, NasimeSabz.com, said in February 2016. "They add it to keep you from visiting my site."

Ms. Aghdam's personal website included graphic photos of slaughtered animals and pleas not to wear fur jackets or have sex outside of marriage. More recently, she focused on what she perceived as discrimination by YouTube and Google. Ms. Aghdam had YouTube pages in Persian, Turkish and English.

In February 2017, she criticized YouTube in a video on Facebook for restricting one of her workout videos to older audiences. "This is what they are doing to vegan activists and many other people who try to promote healthy, humane and smart living — people like me are not good for big business, like for animal business, medicine business and for many other businesses. That's why they are discriminating and censoring us," she said in the video.

By Tuesday night, YouTube, Instagram and Facebook had all taken down her pages and videos. Ed Barberini, San Bruno's police chief, said on Wednesday that investigators were aware of Ms. Aghdam's criticism of YouTube and Google.

"We are learning that Ms. Aghdam had a problem with the policies or practices that YouTube had employed," Chief Barberini said in an interview on ABC's "Good Morning America." "Obviously, she was upset."

ACTIVE SHOOTINGS RARELY INVOLVE WOMEN

Active shooting incidents in the United States are increasingly common, but shootings by women are quite rare.

A 2014 F.B.I. study of 160 active shooting incidents found that at least six involved a woman. Women were involved in three other incidents from 2014 to 2016, according to the bureau. The bureau defined such incidents as "an individual engaging in killing or attempting to kill people in a confined and populated area," and distinguished the events from murders or mass killings.

Mass shootings are often regarded as incidents where at least four people are killed.

The most recent mass casualty event involving a woman was the 2015 attack in San Bernardino, Calif., when Tashfeen Malik and her husband Syed Rizwan Farook attacked his co-workers during a holiday party. Fourteen people were killed, and many more were wounded.

In 2010, a woman who had been fired from her job at a Publix Supermarket in Florida returned to the store with a gun. In another instance the same year, a woman shot at co-workers after she had been suspended from her position at Kraft Foods in Philadelphia. Both women had handguns.

Although Ms. Aghdam appeared to have a long-running grudge against YouTube, the police said that it did not appear that she knew any of the three shooting victims.

THOMAS ERDBRINK, **NELLIE BOWLES** and **JACK NICAS** contributed reporting.
DORIS BURKE contributed research.

YouTube Attacker's Complaints Echoed Fight Over Ad Dollars

BY NELLIE BOWLES AND JACK NICAS | APRIL 4, 2018

SAN FRANCISCO — The authorities believe a woman who shot three people at YouTube's headquarters before killing herself on Tuesday was angered by the social media outlet's policies.

While the police did not specifically say what those policies were, they likely had to do with a concept called "demonetization." In response to pressure from advertisers and consumers, YouTube has been pulling ads from thousands of videos that it decides do not meet its standards for content. That has sparked an outcry from many of the people who post videos to the service.

One of those creators was Nasim Najafi Aghdam, the woman the police said had shot YouTube employees in San Bruno, Calif. She frequently posted videos to several YouTube channels and had become increasingly angry over the money she was making from them.

"My Revenue For 300,000 Views Is $0.10?????" Ms. Aghdam wrote on her website, while calling YouTube "a dictatorship." "There is no equal growth opportunity on YOUTUBE or any other video sharing site, your channel will grow if they want to!!!!!"

Ms. Aghdam's complaints echoed what a wide range of YouTube posters — from self-described animal rights activists like her to right-wing political provocateurs — have increasingly been protesting over the last year.

When YouTube was started in 2005, it took a hands-off approach to much of what was posted, so long as the content was not overly violent or sexual. In 2012, YouTube began allowing almost any video to carry ads, enabling advertisers to reach consumers where they were on the internet. It also gave video creators, from commercial giants to one person recording on a laptop computer, a way to make money off their work.

JIM WILSON/THE NEW YORK TIMES

YouTube's headquarters on Wednesday. In response to pressure from advertisers and consumers, YouTube has been pulling ads from thousands of videos that it decides do not meet its standards for content.

But a series of news reports revealed big brands' ads running alongside extremist, racist and other hateful videos, leading some companies to pull their money from the site. YouTube has since clamped down and pulled ads from thousands of controversial videos.

YouTube declined to comment on Wednesday.

Video creators take a share of the money from ads running before or alongside their videos. But YouTube has been raising the bar on qualifications for running ads.

Last April, the company said it would set a requirement for 10,000 cumulative lifetime views before allowing videos to gain ads. In January, the company raised that requirement to 4,000 hours of watch time in the past year and 1,000 subscribers.

When YouTube pulls ads, it tells creators which videos violated the standards, though it doesn't elaborate very much on what they did wrong. It's unclear whether YouTube pulled ads from Ms. Aghdam's videos.

The anger around demonetization has been growing for more than a year.

One of YouTube's most popular personalities, Felix Arvid Ulf Kjellberg, who goes by PewDiePie, posted videos with Nazi imagery, including a sign that called for "Death to Jews." As a punishment, YouTube demonetized some of his videos in early 2017, though it didn't outrightly bar him. Mr. Kjellberg, now calling himself "family-friendly," still posts regularly and has a booming business on the platform.

In December, YouTube's chief executive, Susan Wojcicki, said the company would hire 10,000 people to enforce company policies regarding videos.

Around that time, another YouTube star, Logan Paul, posted video of himself nervously laughing at the dead body of a man who appeared to have committed suicide. The company again had to apologize and announced that it was removing Mr. Paul from its top-tier payment system and canceling plans to pay him to make a show.

Ms. Wojcicki said in January that YouTube was looking to hire an even bigger team of monitors to look more closely at the platform's content and decide what should belong.

A wide spectrum of YouTube creators, from the conspiracy-minded to the most popular stars, have been vocal about what they see as censorship on YouTube.

After a popular video blogger who posts about news, Philip DeFranco, saw his videos demonetized, he called demonetization "censorship with a different name." On Twitter, he wrote: "Producer just got off the phone with Youtube and it wasn't a mistake. Feels a little bit like getting stabbed in the back after 10 years."

Luke Rudkowski, an independent journalist who describes conspiracy theories to his more than 500,000 subscribers on YouTube, has repeatedly complained about the site pulling ads from his videos.

In August, he posted a video criticizing news that YouTube would start removing more terrorist content. "We are seeing the purging, the cleaning of this major online institution to be more favorable towards corporations and governments," Mr. Rudkowski said. "Now that's why I think we're finally reaching the end time of this beautiful and amazing platform."

A few days later, he said YouTube had pulled ads from 660 of his videos, "basically eviscerating my main source of revenue for this news organization."

Mr. Rudkowski has continued to upload videos to his YouTube channel, WeAreChange, every few days. In a message on Wednesday, he distanced himself and other YouTube creators from Ms. Aghdam.

"In my opinion she was failing and blaming Youtube for her problems," he said. "I dont think its actually about being censored but more about a delusional woman who couldn't accept failure."

On her own website, Ms. Aghdam frequently complained about YouTube's policies, influence and employee politics. In particular she said her animal-rights activism made her a target for scrutiny. She included another video, called "I'm being censored. YouTube's war against vegans," made by the video blogger Emily Moran Barwick, who runs a site called Bite Size Vegan.

Ms. Aghdam posted a video claiming that YouTube had set age restrictions, which would require many viewers to be over 18 years old, on a workout video even though videos from pop stars like Nicki Minaj were much more provocative. And she believed that YouTube's parent company, Google, was targeting her.

"When searching for my website in google, at top of link they add 'an error occurred' but there is no error!" she wrote on her site in February 2016. "They add it to keep you from visiting my site."

CHAPTER 6

Selling Out or Cashing In?

Influencers with large numbers of followers can earn large sums from businesses eager to reach that audience. While many influencers have grown their follower numbers organically, others have sought the easy way to get them by paying for them. Influencers can also have their revenue streams restricted, whether it's done directly by a platform because of content that does not meet their standards or indirectly by plummeting subscriber numbers in the wake of a "cancellation."

Selling a Celebrity Look

BY CLAIRE CAIN MILLER | FEB. 21, 2010

THE PAPARAZZI TRACKED down Angelina Jolie and four of her children in Venice last week, snapping photos of them eating ice cream. Her fans analyzed the photos, looking for the presence of Brad Pitt, at her new blond highlights and for clues to what she was wearing.

On some blogs, those fans could also click on the clothes or accessories in a photo and buy a French Connection scarf, J. Crew wool coat or Luella oversize sunglasses similar to those Ms. Jolie wore.

Fashion lovers have always scoured magazines about gossip and fashion to steal trendy ideas from the rich and famous. (And fashion magazines have long maintained that readers view ads as news.) The Internet has made it easier for readers to shop for celebrities' looks, and it has the added advantage of producing advertising and a little e-commerce revenue in the process.

Readers click on or scroll over a celebrity photo on sites like JustJared, INFDaily or CelebStyle to see what kind of clothes Jessica Biel or Nicole Richie are wearing and where to buy them.

Print magazines often list stores where readers can buy the clothes shown in the magazine, but they appear in tiny print in the back. Identifying items celebrities wear has been a popular feature on fashion blogs and the Web sites of magazines like Lucky and InStyle, but they do it with only a handful of photos. And very few use it as a way to bolster e-commerce and advertising revenue.

"On sites that allow you to shop the look, it's easy — it's just one click and it's done," said Kathryn Finney, founder of Simply Good Media, which has four shopping blogs. "It obviously gives them an advantage."

Companies like GumGum and Pixazza tag the paparazzi photos with links for buying the clothes. They hire people to look at photos and match the clothes they are wearing with the same or similar, more affordable items from retailers like Bloomingdale's, Nordstrom and Zappos. (Image recognition technology is not yet sophisticated enough to automate the process, they say.) The companies get a small fee from retailers when a shopper clicks on or buys an article of clothing.

"Publishers and readers look at it as this really informational resource," said Ophir Tanz, chief executive of GumGum, which tagged the photo of Ms. Jolie with one of its "Shop this look" badges. "We look at it as an ad unit."

Celebrity sites are an obvious place to start with this business, but photos all over the Web could be turned into ads or e-commerce portals, said Bob Lisbonne, chief executive of Pixazza. Pixazza plans to add sites that cover travel, sports and interior design.

"Twenty percent of Web real estate is image space, and it's not really monetized well at all," he said.

The idea is attracting investors looking for a new way to advertise to readers online. Pixazza has raised $5.8 million from investors, including Google Ventures, and GumGum has raised $3.9 million from First Round Capital and others.

Sugar Inc., which publishes celebrity gossip and fashion blogs, was being flooded with reader e-mail messages asking what celebrities were wearing in pictures, so it started a site that gives this information called CelebStyle. When readers click or buy, Sugar gets a small payment from the retailer. CelebStyle plans to do the same with photos of room interiors, said Lisa Sugar, editor in chief of Sugar.

Blog readers seem to like the additional information. People click on "Shop this look" badges 5 to 15 times as often as they click on other Web ads, Mr. Tanz said.

How good a business proposition celebrity fashion photos are remains to be seen. Though many people look at the outfits, it is not clear how many buy the clothes from the sites. Even when they do, the publishers and ad companies receive only a small fraction of the sale.

Kate Mitchell, 27, works in technical support in Denver and peruses gossip blogs to get fashion ideas from celebrities, but she rarely makes a purchase. Instead, she uses the ideas to come up with new ways to wear things she already owns, she said.

She recently saw a photo of Kate Winslet walking down the street in a navy shift dress with a white cardigan. "I was so excited because I was like, 'I own that dress and it was like $40,' " she said. She recreated the outfit.

Yet even if a picture with a GumGum or Pixazza ad does not result in a sale, a celebrity's endorsement by choosing to carry a certain designer's handbag to the grocery store can be invaluable to the brand, retailers say.

Singer22, a retailer, makes sure blogs know when a celebrity wears something it sells. "It's brand recognition," said its owner, Jon Singer. "We're this place that sells clothes that celebrities wear."

CelebStyle receives daily e-mail messages from brands like Louis

Vuitton and Paige Premium Denim, alerting the site that a celebrity is wearing one of their items in a photo on Sugar's other blogs, Alexis Lerch, editor of CelebStyle, said.

Joey Ly, 28, a controller at a Philadelphia hotel, recently bought a Gustto handbag for $645 after seeing a photo online of Halle Berry carrying it, though she went to another site to buy it. "I definitely bought the bag based on the fact that Halle Berry had the same bag," Ms. Ly said.

Buying Their Way to Twitter Fame

BY AUSTIN CONSIDINE | AUG. 22, 2012

AS A COMEDIAN, Dan Nainan was blessed with fans, millions of YouTube views and, once, an audience with President Obama. But one thing was missing.

"The number of Twitter followers I had in relation to how many people in the world know about me was woefully inadequate," he said. So in June he bought a small city's worth for $424.15, raising his Twitter follower count from about 700 to more than 220,000.

"There's a tremendous cachet associated with having a large number," said Mr. Nainan, 31, adding later, "When people see that you have that many followers, they're like: 'Oh, my goodness, this guy is popular. I might want to book him.' "

It may be the worst-kept secret in the Twittersphere. That friend who brags about having 1,000, even 100,000 Twitter followers may not have earned them through hard work and social networking; he may have simply bought them on the black market.

And it's not just ego-driven blogger types. Celebrities, politicians, start-ups, aspiring rock stars, reality show hopefuls — anyone who might benefit from having a larger social media footprint — are known to have bought large blocks of Twitter followers.

The practice is surprisingly easy. A Google search for "buy Twitter followers" turns up dozens of Web sites like USocial.net, InterTwitter.com, and FanMeNow.com that sell Twitter followers by the thousands (and often Facebook likes and YouTube views). At BuyTwitterFollow.com, for example, users simply enter their Twitter handle and credit card number and, with a few clicks, see the ranks of their followers swell in three to four days.

Will Mitchell, the founder of Clear Presence Media, a marketing company outside Tampa, Fla., said that he has bought more than a

CHRISTOPH HITZ

million followers for his clients, which include musicians, start-ups and a well-known actress he declined to identify.

"And it's so cheap, too," he said. In one instance, Mr. Mitchell said, he bought 250,000 for $2,500, or a penny each.

One site, Fiverr, an online classified for cheap marketing services, has several ads offering 1,000 Twitter followers for $5.

Heddi Cundle, founder of MyTab.co, a San Francisco company that helps people raise money for trips, spent $5 on Fiverr to buy 200 followers last October, when her site started. By the next month, "we had about 1,100 to 1,200 people on both Twitter and Facebook, which was amazing," she said. "We needed that to get ourselves going."

Fake Twitter followers briefly made the news in July, when Mitt Romney's Twitter following jumped by more than 100,000 in one weekend — a much faster rate than usual. A flurry of news reports purported to expose the practice of buying followers. "Romney Twitter account gets upsurge in fake followers, but from where?" read a headline on the NBC News Technolog blog." (The Romney campaign has denied it bought followers.) Similar claims were lobbed at Newt Gingrich last year; his campaign also denied that he paid for any of his 1.3 million-strong Twitter following.

Having fake followers, it is important to note, does not necessarily mean that they were purchased. Unlike Facebook friends, Twitter does not require users to approve followers. In other words, anyone can follow you on Twitter, whether it's your mother or a spammer.

Twitter followers are sold in two ways: "Targeted" followers, as they are known in the industry, are harvested using software that seeks out Twitter users with similar interests and follows them, betting that many will return the favor. "Generated" followers are from Twitter accounts that are either inactive or created by spamming computers — often referred to as "bots."

Buyers and sellers see nothing wrong with it. "Buying followers generated by bots is against Twitter's terms and frowned upon by the public," Mr. Mitchell said. "However, it is perfectly legal."

The practice has become so widespread that StatusPeople, a social media management company in London, released a Web tool last month called the Fake Follower Check that it says can ascertain how many fake followers you and your friends have.

The tool examines Twitter relationships, said Rob Waller, a founder of StatusPeople. "Fake accounts tend to follow a lot of people but have few followers," he said. "We then combine that with a few other metrics to confirm the account is fake."

If accurate, the number of fake followers out there is surprising. According to the StatusPeople tool, 71 percent of Lady Gaga's nearly 29 million followers are "fake" or "inactive." So are 70 percent of President Obama's nearly 19 million followers.

But Twitter is starting to clamp down. In April, it filed suit in federal court in San Francisco against five spammers, including those who create fake Twitter followers. (The case is pending.) That didn't

EMILY BERL FOR THE NEW YORK TIMES

Dan Nainan performing during his standup comedy class last night at the American Comedy Institute in Manhattan.

discourage Mr. Nainan, the comedian. He recently asked about "the theoretical maximum" Twitter followers he can purchase.

"They said, 'You could probably get over a million, a million and a half,' " he said. "And I'm like, 'Why not? I can afford it.' "

The Well-Followed on Social Media Cash In on Their Influence

BY JENNA WORTHAM | JUNE 8, 2014

GOOD THING SOCIAL MEDIA did not exist during the era of "Mad Men." It might have put Don and Peggy out of business.

Brands and advertisers, looking for ways to reach audiences beyond television screens and magazine pages, are turning to people with many followers on social media and paying them to pitch products online. The social media stars, in turn, are finding that working as a conduit for a brand can be quite lucrative — sometimes generating more than enough money to live on.

Robby Ayala, for example, dropped out of law school to pursue his career as a full-time video creator on the video service Vine, publishing several goofy six-second movies to his 2.6 million followers each day. Last summer, he got a call from Niche, a company that wanted to hire him to make a short commercial for GroupMe, a messaging application, and post it for his followers to see.

Mr. Ayala, a natural ham, made a short comedy skit of himself using GroupMe to text his friends a selfie photo. He accepted the job, and others like it, which pay several thousand dollars, and he has not looked back since.

"I saw how it could be more of a profession than a hobby," he said. "I wanted to be a part of it all."

Mr. Ayala and others like him have joined a long line of innovators who have found clever ways to build businesses on top of existing websites and platforms — often before the services themselves have figured out how to make money. The early days of the iPhone, Facebook and Twitter, for example, were defined by the applications built by developers for those products and services.

This latest incarnation follows the tradition. Only this time, advertisers are tapping popular personalities and characters on Vine,

SANDY HUFFAKER FOR THE NEW YORK TIMES

Jethro Ames making a stop-motion video in his garage studio.

owned by Twitter, to make microcommercials in the same spirit and style that made the social media account popular in the first place.

Mr. Ayala made a name for himself on Vine by filming humorous skits with his friends and family that made use of his boyish good looks and physical comedy. In November, Mr. Ayala joined Niche full time, to work as the company's creative partnership manager, which he described as helping other Vine users polish their content and make videos for advertisers.

In many ways, Niche has become a talent scouting service and advertising agency rolled up into one — it matches social media stars with marketers and advertisers who want to reach the young users who inhabit those platforms full time. Those users then make content — like Instagram images or Vine shorts — around a company or product, like baby clothes or a sports drink, and post it to their accounts for their followers to like and comment on.

Niche says that it has close to 3,000 social media accounts, with a total reach of 500 million followers. The agency has worked with roughly 70 brands, including Home Depot, General Electric and Gap Kids.

Liz Jones, executive vice president for digital marketing at Relativity EuropaCorp Distribution, a media company that produces feature films and television shows, said that Niche was just one outlet of many that she used to market her company's offerings.

Ms. Jones turned to Niche recently when she wanted to market a coming children's movie, "Earth to Echo."

The company flew a handful of popular users on Vine and Instagram to meet the stars of the film and post about it on their various social media accounts.

The company wanted to reach young users "in a way that's really in their world, rather than just with our regular ads," she said.

And she wanted to make sure that "Echo," which had no boldface-name stars, did not go unnoticed by her target demographic.

"I'm a big believer in that influencer marketer," she said, "or someone telling you that something is cool and that you should like it."

The resulting Vines and Instagrams directly correlated to spikes in traffic to the film's Wikipedia page and views of the trailer on YouTube, she said, and that is what she had hoped for.

"That's all I wanted to do at that point," she said. "Just spark their interest so that if they don't know about the movie, they look it up and are talking about it."

Rob Fishman, one of the founders of Niche, described the service as a "native ad factory," referring to the kinds of advertisements that look somewhat similar to the content around them.

"It's not canned content; it looks and feels like the native content in their native feeds," he said.

Native advertising is one of the fastest-growing types of advertising, especially on mobile devices. The format has raised questions from federal regulators about how paid content that blurs the line between editorial content and ads should be identified to users.

OZIER MUHAMMAD/THE NEW YORK TIMES

Rob Fishman, a founder of Niche, in its New York offices. Niche matches social media stars with marketers and advertisers.

The government already requires that sponsored posts, paid search results and promoted posts must be denoted as such, but has not yet set additional guidelines. Many expect that it will do so, to help consumers distinguish between regular posts and advertisements.

In the case of Niche, posts usually include a comment or hashtag referring to the company they are promoting for their followers, but there is no mention that the video is an advertisement. Mr. Fishman said that the company encouraged social media celebrities who participate in promotions to use language like "I'm partnering with" or "teaming up with" or even hashtags like #sponsored or #ad to help consumers distinguish between them.

Jethro Ames, 35, who lives in San Diego, described himself as a "traditional print designer" who built a career on print ads and logos when he started making stop-motion videos and posting them on Vine. Eventually, the demand for his stylistic Vines outpaced his traditional print work, and he quit to work on social media full time. He even transformed the two-car garage in his home into a production studio for his social media creations.

Many of his videos are posted by the brand account he works for, like Home Depot, making it clear they are promoting the company.

"People don't sit around watching prime-time TV waiting for ads to appear anymore," he said. "They watch online or even through the Twittersphere. It's powerful."

Mr. Fishman says that campaigns through Niche pay a broad range of fees, from $500 to as much as $50,000, but the average payout for a Vine campaign ranges in the mid-four figures. Mr. Ames declined to say how much he earned, but said people posting advertisements on Vine can make six figures a year, and some as much as $300,000.

Niche itself makes money, too, Mr. Fishman said. The company, which has a few more than a dozen employees split between San Francisco and New York, has generated more than $1.5 million in revenue since its inception last June and expects to bring in over $4 million by the end of the year.

The company recently raised $2.5 million in venture financing from SoftTech, Lerer Ventures and SV Angel, among others, at an $11 million valuation.

Mr. Fishman said he and Darren Lachtman, Niche's other co-founder, hoped to create the future of advertising on mobile phones.

Companies "don't have to pay to hire Don Draper" for expensive print and television ads, he said. "They can come to us to create it."

Now You Can Just Pay Celebrities to Say Stuff

CRITIC'S NOTEBOOK | BY AMANDA HESS | AUG. 1, 2018

Cameo is the "Being John Malkovich" of apps.

REMEMBER NIKKI BLONSKY? She was the unknown Long Island teen plucked from a Cold Stone Creamery and cast as the star of the 2007 movie musical "Hairspray." Now, a decade after that big splash, her acting career has slowed to a drip. Recently she lent her voice to "Pup Star," a direct-to-digital entry in the "Air Bud" extended universe. Soon she'll appear in a horror movie opposite Gary Busey's son. But lately Ms. Blonsky has found a new performance platform: Cameo, a service that allows fans to pay low- to midrange celebrities to send them short, personalized video messages.

Ms. Blonsky is the bard of Cameo. She excels at the projection of intimacy. She takes a few spare details about her subject — an upcoming birthday, a career milestone — and spins them into a sugar-voiced pep talk filmed as a dim, shaky selfie. The heady mix of heartfelt emoting and janky video quality creates the illusion of a bridged gap between celebrity and fan. The experience costs $20.

Cameo is an intriguing new development in celebrity-fan relations. Commoners have always had a tenuous relationship with the stars. Their images and life stories exert a strong gravitational pull over our own, and the internet has provided the opportunity for the masses to yank back. Attempting to assert control in the confines of celebrity culture can take the form of fanatical image monitoring (as is the case with celebrity Photoshop-obsessed communities like Pretty Ugly Little Liar); creepy body fixations (indexing and cataloging celebrity parts on sites like WikiFeet and CelebHeights.com); erotic fan fiction (where you can write your favorite star into any scenario you choose); and criminal invasions (hacking and trading nude images).

Cameo offers something new. It's a kind of celebrity ventriloquism — the opportunity to project your voice through a famous host. It's the "Being John Malkovich" of apps.

Here's how it works: Browse an array of available Cameo "talent" — the list includes "The O.C." star Mischa Barton (current rate: $75), the N.F.L. Hall-of-Famer Terrell Owens ($350), the former boy-bander Lance Bass ($125) and a raft of "Real Housewives" socialites — and choose your favorite player. Then type in some credit card information and a set of instructions.

The dummy copy reads: "My buddy Shia (pronounced SHY-UH) is graduating from college on Saturday (my name is Jason). Played football with him for three years, loves all your content. Our favorite saying is 'okay pal?'. Please wish him a happy graduation."

If the celebrity accepts the request, a video will materialize in your inbox within a week. If he or she doesn't, you'll receive a sad GIF and won't be charged. Cameo "talent" is free to reject any request found "confusing, difficult, or not in line with an athlete's or influencer's image," so the potential thrill of being recognized by a B-list celebrity always comes with the risk of being rebuffed by one.

Steven Galanis, a former LinkedIn account executive who is C.E.O. of Cameo, realized a couple years ago that "the celebrity selfie is the new autograph" and set out to democratize the experience with the help of co-founders Devon Townsend, a former Microsoft engineer, and Martin Blencowe, a producer and N.F.L. agent. Now, you no longer need to hope for a random celebrity run-in to secure such an image; you can pay Cameo to engineer it for you.

But Mr. Galanis's even-more-valuable intuition was this: Famous people are willing to do a lot more for money than was previously assumed. Mr. Galanis recalled asking the New York Knicks player Lance Thomas, a friend of his from college, how much it would cost for him to make an appearance at a Long Island bar mitzvah, and he replied, "Bro, I'll go anywhere for $2,000."

Mr. Galanis did the math: Maybe three hours at the event, plus one hour of travel each way, amounted to about six dollars a minute. But boil an "appearance" down to just the few minutes it takes to shoot a video, and such experiences could be made available on a wide scale — "the greatest gift ever, and cheaper than a ticket to a Knicks game," Mr. Galanis said. Mr. Thomas is now a Cameo investor and on its talent roster.

Along the way, Cameo has unwittingly created a new style of performance. Some practitioners are more skilled than others. Occasionally, requested messages enter the celebrity's brain and come out garbled. Others just seem insincere.

Even a "bad" Cameo offers something of value, which is a totally new way of analyzing a celebrity persona. Dina Lohan, best known for giving birth to Lindsay, has struggled to adapt to the form. In her Cameos, she regularly appears perched in a striped armchair next to an enormous silk curtain contraption, filmed from across the room by an unseen handler. Her messages come off as scripted and rote, which, of course, they are. She has received such feedback from users as "She said 31st birthday instead of 35th" and "She doesn't seem to be having fun." But there's also something wonderful about receiving a text message containing an artifact like this. It's like a direct injection of her arid momager essence.

A few celebrities appear to be using Cameo as a one-on-one image rehabilitation service. When I requested a Cameo from Jon Gosselin of "Jon & Kate Plus Eight," he made sure to casually drop this: "I'm so busy I had to do it from my car." $40.

Rebecca Black, who rose to infamy as an awkward teenager in 2011, when a low-budget music video for her puzzling and atonal single, "Friday" went viral, has re-emerged on Cameo, where she seems to have found her calling. Now 21, she is suddenly gorgeous and self-assured. In her videos, she appears winkingly gracious to her "fans" for listening to "Friday," then performs a twee ukulele version. Her voice sounds amazing. $30.

One of the most intriguing aspects of Cameo is not the videos but the site itself, where famous people from every corner of modern celebrity — music, sports, YouTube, reality TV, viral infamy — assign a dollar amount to their self-worth. Celebrities set their own rates; Cameo takes a 25 percent cut. The real-life "Wolf of Wall Street" Jordan Belfort has offered himself up for $1,000. Mr. Owens once charged $500 but has since dropped his rate to $350. The model Adriana Lima (who has the same name as a Victoria's Secret model) costs $40. Lee Garrett, a former "Bachelorette" contestant perhaps best known for his racist comments, goes for $5.

In addition to soliciting Cameos from Ms. Blonsky and Mr. Gosselin, I bought videos from the celebrity gossip Perez Hilton, the youth culture queen Bella Thorne and Ms. Lohan. Because I am a sadist, I asked them to say "Peter Piper picked a peck of pickled peppers." They mostly did, and now I feel strangely tender toward them all.

Except for Ms. Lohan. Instead of repeating the tongue twister, she sat in her chair, told "me," I guess, that she had just returned from opening Lohan Beach Clubs in Greece, and wished my family "love, laughter, and great health." She didn't say my name. $75.

AMANDA HESS is a critic-at-large. She writes about internet culture for the Arts section and contributes regularly to The New York Times Magazine. She has written for such publications as Slate, ESPN the Magazine, Elle and Pacific Standard.

YouTube Drops Online Star Logan Paul From Premium Advertising

BY DAISUKE WAKABAYASHI | JAN. 10, 2018

SAN FRANCISCO — YouTube said on Wednesday that it had dropped Logan Paul, one of its most popular stars, from its top advertising ranks and had suspended production of a YouTube movie that he was supposed to appear in.

Late last month, Mr. Paul faced a deluge of criticism after posting a video that appeared to show a dead body hanging from a tree in a Japanese forest known as a destination for suicides. Mr. Paul took the video down and apologized for what he called a "misguided" decision.

The move to punish Mr. Paul a week after the video surfaced highlights how YouTube, which is owned by Google, is slowly coming to grips with controversial content. The issue is becoming more apparent as the online service replaces television as the main entertainment platform for younger audiences.

Top YouTube stars like Mr. Paul, known for pushing the envelope with outlandish behavior that would not be acceptable on mainstream television, present a particular problem. Their antics build an online audience, but can create a cycle of boundary testing as they look for ways to keep their viewers entertained.

"In light of recent events," said a YouTube spokeswoman, Jessica Mason, Mr. Paul was dropped from Google Preferred, which grants content creators access to guaranteed revenue from premium advertisers. She also said YouTube was delaying any projects that it had in the works with Mr. Paul, including a sequel to a YouTube movie called "The Thinning."

YouTube had been criticized for not taking stronger action against Mr. Paul. The company had issued a statement saying it prohibited gory or violent videos on the platform and it offered condolences to the family of the young man seen in the video.

Few YouTube stars have built a following more successfully than Mr. Paul. With floppy blond hair, a muscular physique and an easy-going personality, Mr. Paul has 15.7 million followers for his vlog — a daily video that is a cross between a diary and a reality show.

Mr. Paul's popularity has moved beyond YouTube. He is expected to star in a romantic comedy musical movie called "Valley Girl" later this year, has created songs that have jumped to the top of iTunes charts, and is selling his own Maverick branded merchandise.

Mr. Paul has not posted a vlog in a week since he posted an apology video. A spokeswoman for him did not respond immediately to a request for comment.

Last year, YouTube dropped another one of its stars, Felix Kjellberg, better known by his YouTube alias PewDiePie, from its top-tier advertising after reports surfaced about anti-Semitic comments he made on video.

James Charles, From 'CoverBoy' to Canceled

BY VALERIYA SAFRONOVA | MAY 14, 2019

The 19-year-old internet personality and makeup artist has provoked the ire of beauty YouTube.

WHEN JAMES CHARLES, 19, became the first male face of CoverGirl, following in the steps of household names like Tyra Banks, Taylor Swift and Katy Perry, he was just a high school senior. In his hometown, Bethlehem, N.Y., he would charge friends between $5 and $10 to do their makeup for special occasions and had amassed a few hundred thousand Instagram followers by posting his eye-catching D.I.Y. beauty looks.

In the few years since, he has become an internet sensation in the beauty world, with 16 million YouTube subscribers (and nearly the same number on Instagram), his own merchandise line and makeup partnerships, and a devoted following. He recently attended this year's camp-themed Met Gala, the biggest party in fashion.

In a matter of days, everything changed. Mr. Charles is now at the center of an ongoing debate about betrayal among a passionate group of beauty vloggers, bona fide celebrities and the meme-makers of TikTok. He has lost about three million followers on YouTube; Miley Cyrus, Shawn Mendes and Kylie Jenner have all unfollowed him on Instagram.

On Friday, Tati Westbrook, 37, a YouTube beauty vlogger and a former mentor to Mr. Charles, posted a video in which she told Mr. Charles, as well as several million of her closest subscribers, that she no longer wants anything to do with him. Ms. Westbrook, who owns a vitamin company, described in detail how an Instagram ad that Mr. Charles posted on behalf of a rival supplement's company was a betrayal of their friendship. The summary of the video also links to her product site, Halo Beauty.

KRISTA SCHLUETER FOR THE NEW YORK TIMES

James Charles at Gucci's Met Gala after-party on May 6. In the week since, he lost millions of YouTube subscribers after another influencer, Tati Westbrook, shared a critical video about him.

She said that she was also upset by Mr. Charles's attempt to "trick a straight man into thinking he's gay, yet again," an incident she said happened at her most recent birthday celebration.

"He's 19 and I'm afraid of him," Ms. Westbrook said at the end of the video, which has been viewed more than 40 million times. Mr. Charles posted a barefaced apology video that same day, but the two have not publicly reconciled.

The beauty-influencer world is one in which interpersonal conflicts often play out in videos posted across YouTube channels, with players flinging accusations at each other or apologizing in 15-minute monologues to their fans. The rumor mill they spin into existence is bolstered by coverage from "drama channels," YouTube accounts that keep track of the gossip and "expose" the wrongdoings of various local celebrities.

Receipts are a commodity in this world — not literal receipts that are printed after a purchase, but metaphorical receipts in the form of digital records that are supposed to prove innocence or guilt. (These often manifest as screenshots of private conversations, photos or videos.) When public fights break out, receipts are "stacked" and, eventually, someone is canceled.

What does a cancellation look like? Mr. Charles is learning.

In the days since Ms. Westbrook posted her video, he has also seen a rapid drop in his YouTube subscriber count, from about 16.5 million to 13.5 million, according to Social Blade, which compiles social media data.

His social media channels have been flooded with negative comments, and former fans have posted short videos on TikTok, in which they find myriad ways to vandalize Mr. Charles's Morphe palette. One dropped the palette into a bathtub full of water. Another painted a snake over the compact's logo. Still another painted, in what appears to be Wite-Out, the words "Bye Sister" — a reference to the title of the Ms. Westbrook's video.

Other members of the "influencer community" have stepped into the fray to defend Mr. Charles or to add to Ms. Westbrook's accusations. Jeffree Star, who has been canceled in the past for saying racist things that he later called "disgusting, vile and nasty," said in a tweet that Mr. Charles "is a danger to society. Everything Tati said is 100% true." (He later deleted the tweet.)

Felix Kjellberg, better known as PewDiePie, a YouTube celebrity with more subscribers than Mr. Charles, Mr. Star and Ms. Westbrook combined, chimed in to question Ms. Westbrook's actions on his channel. "Tati is 37 years old," Mr. Kjellberg said. "James Charles is still a teenager." He added: "For a mother figure to just completely drag this kid — no one has a problem with this?"

The website that sells Mr. Charles's branded merchandise, Sisters Apparel, appeared defunct on Tuesday; fans speculated that Mr. Star had a hand in the shutdown. (Mr. Star is an owner of Killer Merch, a company that designs, manufactures and ships merchandise for brands, including, until recently, Sisters Apparel.)

This is not the first time a storm of controversy has raged around Mr. Charles. In 2017, Mr. Charles tweeted "I can't believe we're going to Africa today omg what if we get Ebola?" He followed the tweet with a Notes app apology in which he referred to Africa as a country.

The incident turned out to be a blip in Mr. Charles's rise. For a couple of months, his YouTube subscriptions slowed down, but by May of that year, it was back up to hundreds of thousands per month and kept growing afterward. Even over the last few days, though Mr. Charles's subscriber count has plummeted, his video views are up and in the millions. His 8-minute apology video, for example, has more than 40 million views.

VALERIYA SAFRONOVA is a reporter for the Style section. She is based in New York.

Glossary

algorithm A step-by-step procedure for solving a problem or accomplishing an objective.

amateur Someone who does something for the love of it instead of for money.

analytics The analysis of statistics or data.

anti-Semitic Showing hostility toward or prejudice against Jewish people.

canceled Dismissed, either wholly or in part, particularly on a social media platform.

capitalize To make money off of; to profit from.

cyberbullying To bully people on the Internet.

Douyin (TikTok) A Chinese live-streaming site.

Generation Z The generation of people born in the mid-1990s and early 2000s.

hashtag A phrase or word preceded by a number sign that is used on social media sites to indicate the topic of the message.

Internet famous Someone who is famous on the Internet but not in other entertainment circles.

kidfluencer A child who gains a large following online.

live-stream An event that is transmitted live over the Internet.

meme A humorous video, image or snippet of text that spreads rapidly throughout the Internet.

millennials The generation of people born in the early 1980s and early 1990s.

predatory Behavior that preys on humans or animals.

radicalization The process of a person adopting extreme positions on social or political issues.

Rickrolling A prank in which a person is linked to a music video that features Rick Astley's "Never Gonna Give You Up."

social media influencer An individual with a large following of viewers on the Internet who typically has gained credibility in a particular industry.

unboxing A video of a person opening a new product's box.

viral When content on the Internet is shared widely.

vlog Short videos that appear on a social media account or website.

WeChat A Chinese messenger app.

Weibo China's most popular microblogging site.

Media Literacy Terms

"Media literacy" refers to the ability to access, understand, critically assess and create media. The following terms are important components of media literacy, and they will help you critically engage with the articles in this title.

angle The aspect of a news story that a journalist focuses on and develops.

attribution The method by which a source is identified or by which facts and information are assigned to the person who provided them.

balance Principle of journalism that both perspectives of an argument should be presented in a fair way.

chronological order Method of writing a story presenting the details of the story in the order in which they occurred.

column A type of story that is a regular feature, often on a recurring topic, written by the same journalist, generally known as a columnist.

commentary A type of story that is an expression of opinion on recent events by a journalist generally known as a commentator.

credibility The quality of being trustworthy and believable, said of a journalistic source.

critical review A type of story that describes an event or work of art, such as a theater performance, film, concert, book, restaurant, radio or television program, exhibition or musical piece, and offers critical assessment of its quality and reception.

editorial Article of opinion or interpretation.

human interest story A type of story that focuses on individuals and how events or issues affect their life, generally offering a sense of relatability to the reader.

impartiality Principle of journalism that a story should not reflect a journalist's bias and should contain balance.

intention The motive or reason behind something, such as the publication of a news story.

interview story A type of story in which the facts are gathered primarily by interviewing another person or persons.

motive The reason behind something, such as the publication of a news story or a source's perspective on an issue.

news story An article or style of expository writing that reports news, generally in a straightforward fashion and without editorial comment.

op-ed An opinion piece that reflects a prominent individual's opinion on a topic of interest.

paraphrase The summary of an individual's words, with attribution, rather than a direct quotation of their exact words.

quotation The use of an individual's exact words indicated by the use of quotation marks and proper attribution.

reliability The quality of being dependable and accurate, said of a journalistic source.

rhetorical device Technique in writing intending to persuade the reader or communicate a message from a certain perspective.

source The origin of the information reported in journalism.

style A distinctive use of language in writing or speech; also a news or publishing organization's rules for consistent use of language with regards to spelling, punctuation, typography and capitalization, usually regimented by a house style guide.

tone A manner of expression in writing or speech.

Media Literacy Questions

1. Identify the various sources cited in the article "Finding Fame, and Sometimes Fortune, in Social Media" (on page 17). How does Steven Leckart attribute information to each of his sources? How effective are Leckart's attributions in helping the reader identify his sources?

2. What type of story is "ILoveMakonnen Is Big Online and Almost Famous" (on page 51)? Can you identify another article in this collection that is the same type of story? What elements helped you come to your conclusion?

3. Is the article "How Cats Evolved to Win the Internet" (on page 72) a compelling example of an opinion piece? Identify how Abigail Tucker's attitude and tone help convey information about the topic.

4. In "YouTube's Product Chief on Online Radicalization and Algorithmic Rabbit Holes" (on page 110), Kevin Roose interviews YouTube's chief product officer. What approach did Roose take when interviewing the subject? Did the questions seem carefully prepared, or did Roose seem to adapt them naturally as the conversation proceeded? Did Roose succeed in clarifying the material? Was the interview subject clear and upfront, or cagey and reticent when responding to the questions? Why do you think this is?

5. Does "Chinese Censors Have New Target: Celebrity News" (on page 145) use multiple sources? What are the strengths of using multiple sources in a journalistic piece? What are the weaknesses?

6. "PewDiePie Put in Spotlight After New Zealand Shooting" (on page 161) is an article about a violent act and its connection to a social media influencer. Examine the journalist's tone in the piece. Does the reporting seem impartial and balanced? Why or why not?

7. "The Latest Celebrity Diet? Cyberbullying" (on page 171) criticizes the behavior of some social media celebrities. Do you think this criticism is well-supported by Amanda Hess's arguments? Why or why not?

8. What is the intention of the article "Selling a Celebrity Look" (on page 188)? How effectively does it achieve its intended purpose?

9. Often, as a news story develops, a journalist's attitude toward the subject may change. Compare "The Well-Followed on Social Media Cash In on Their Influence" (on page 196) and "Drizzy and the New Celebrity Worship" (on page 57), both by Jenna Wortham. Did Wortham's perspective seem to change between the publication of the two articles? Why or why not?

10. What is the style and tone of "Now You Can Just Pay Celebrities to Say Stuff" (on page 201)? How does this affect the purpose of the article? Why do you think this is?

11. Identify each of the sources in "YouTube Drops Online Star Logan Paul From Premium Advertising" (on page 205) as a primary source or a secondary source. Evaluate the credibility of each source. How does your evaluation change your perspective on this article?

Citations

All citations in this list are formatted according to the Modern Language Association's (MLA) style guide.

BOOK CITATION

THE NEW YORK TIMES EDITORIAL STAFF. *Social Media Influencers: Apps, Algorithms and Celebrities.* New York Times Educational Publishing, 2020.

ONLINE ARTICLE CITATIONS

BARNES, BROOKS. "Coming Soon: Celebrity Web Networks From the Media Company Whalerock." *The New York Times,* 18 Feb. 2015, https://www.nytimes.com/2015/02/18/business/media/coming-soon-web-networks-for-a-bevy-of-celebrities.html.

BARNES, BROOKS. "Hollywood Rushes to VidCon to Connect With Millennials." *The New York Times,* 22 May 2016, https://www.nytimes.com/2016/05/23/business/media/hollywood-rushes-to-vidcon-to-connect-with-millennials.html.

BENNER, KATIE, AND SAPNA MAHESHWARI. "Snapchat Plays Hard to Get With Celebrities and Influencers." *The New York Times,* 18 Dec. 2016, https://www.nytimes.com/2016/12/18/technology/snapchat-plays-hard-to-get-with-celebrities-and-influencers.html.

BILTON, NICK. "At VidCon, Small-Screen Stars and Big-Time Fame." *The New York Times,* 22 July 2015, https://www.nytimes.com/2015/07/23/style/at-vidcon-small-screen-stars-and-big-time-fame.html.

BOWLES, NELLIE, AND JACK NICAS. "YouTube Attacker's Complaints Echoed Fight Over Ad Dollars." *The New York Times,* 4 Apr. 2018, https://www.nytimes.com/2018/04/04/technology/youtube-attacker-demonetization.html.

BROMWICH, JONAH ENGEL. "Logan Paul, YouTube Star, Says Posting Video of Dead Body Was 'Misguided.' " *The New York Times,* 2 Jan. 2018, https://www.nytimes.com/2018/01/02/business/media/logan-paul-youtube.html.

BUCKLEY, CHRIS. "Some of China's Prominent Internet Voices." *The New York Times*, 10 Sept. 2013, https://www.nytimes.com/2013/09/11/world/asia/some-of-chinas-prominent-internet-voices.html.

CHOKSHI, NIRAJ. "PewDiePie Put in Spotlight After New Zealand Shooting." *The New York Times*, 15 Mar. 2019, https://www.nytimes.com/2019/03/15/technology/pewdiepie-new-zealand-shooting.html.

CONSIDINE, AUSTIN. "Twitter Followers For Sale." *The New York Times*, 22 Aug. 2012, https://www.nytimes.com/2012/08/23/fashion/twitter-followers-for-sale.html.

COSCARELLI, JOE. "ILoveMakonnen Is Big Online and Almost Famous." *The New York Times*, 4 Apr. 2015, https://www.nytimes.com/2015/04/05/arts/music/ilovemakonnen-is-big-online-and-almost-famous.html.

EATON, KIT. "The Best Apps for Delivering Celebrity News." *The New York Times*, 24 Feb. 2016, https://www.nytimes.com/2016/02/25/technology/personaltech/the-best-apps-for-delivering-celebrity-news.html.

FRIEDMAN, VANESSA. "The Rise and (Maybe) Fall of Influencers." *The New York Times*, 10 May 2017, https://www.nytimes.com/2017/05/10/fashion/kendall-jenner-fyre-festival-pepsi-bella-hadid-influencers.html.

HERNÁNDEZ, JAVIER C. "Chinese Citizens Evade Internet Censors to Remember Liu Xiaobo." *The New York Times* 14 July 2017, https://www.nytimes.com/2017/07/14/world/asia/china-liu-xiaobo-censorship-internet.html.

HERRMAN, JOHN. "What if Instagram Got Rid of Likes?" *The New York Times*, 31 May 2019, https://www.nytimes.com/2019/05/31/style/are-likes-and-followers-the-problem-with-social-media.html.

HESS, AMANDA. "A Celebrity Z-List? Yes, It Exists." *The New York Times*, 31 Aug. 2016, https://www.nytimes.com/2016/09/01/arts/instagram-celebrities-sofia-richie.html.

HESS, AMANDA. "The Latest Celebrity Diet? Cyberbullying." *The New York Times*, 12 Oct. 2016, https://www.nytimes.com/2016/10/13/arts/celebrities-twitter-instagram-cyberbullying-kardashian-swift.html.

HESS, AMANDA. "Now You Can Just Pay Celebrities to Say Stuff." *The New York Times*, 1 Aug. 2018, https://www.nytimes.com/2018/08/01/arts/cameo-nikki-blonsky-now-you-can-just-pay-celebrities-to-say-stuff.html.

HESS, AMANDA. "Unboxing the Internet for Teens, Eightysomethings and Everyone in Between." *The New York Times*, 21 Nov. 2017, https://www.nytimes.com/2017/11/21/insider/internet-culture-memes-amanda-hess.html.

HIGA, LIRIEL. "We're Living in the World That Klout Built." *The New York Times*, 14 May 2018, https://www.nytimes.com/2018/05/14/opinion/klout-social-media-influencers.html.

LARMER, BROOK. "The Dangerous Politics of Internet Humor in China." *The New York Times*, 26 Oct. 2011, https://www.nytimes.com/2011/10/30/magazine/the-dangerous-politics-of-internet-humor-in-china.html.

LAYDEN, EMILY. "On Facebook, Bullies 'Like' If You Hate." *The New York Times*, 9 Sept. 2012, https://parenting.blogs.nytimes.com/2012/09/09/on-facebook-bullies-like-if-you-hate/.

LECKART, STEVEN. "Finding Fame, and Sometimes Fortune, in Social Media." *The New York Times*, 26 Sept. 2012, https://www.nytimes.com/2012/09/27/technology/personaltech/internet-stars-find-an-audience-in-social-media-tool-kit.html.

LYALL, SARAH. "Site Helps Slighted Stars Feeling Internet's Sting." *The New York Times*, 27 Mar. 2011, https://www.nytimes.com/2011/03/28/world/europe/28icorrect.html.

MAHESHWARI, SAPNA. "Facebook's Version of YouTube Takes Shape With Pranksters, Magicians and Cartoons." *The New York Times*, 16 Dec. 2018, https://www.nytimes.com/2018/12/16/business/media/facebook-watch-advertising.html.

MAHESHWARI, SAPNA. "Online and Making Thousands, at Age 4: Meet the Kidfluencers." *The New York Times*, 1 Mar. 2019, https://www.nytimes.com/2019/03/01/business/media/social-media-influencers-kids.html.

MASOOD, SALMAN. "Qandeel Baloch, Pakistani Social Media Celebrity, Dead in Apparent Honor Killing." *The New York Times*, 16 July 2016, https://www.nytimes.com/2016/07/17/world/asia/qandeel-baloch-pakistan-internet-celebrity-killed.html.

MILLER, CLAIRE CAIN. "Selling a Celebrity Look With a Photo and a Click." *The New York Times*, 21 Feb. 2010, https://www.nytimes.com/2010/02/22/technology/internet/22celebrity.html.

O'LEARY, AMY. "Glued to the Tube." *The New York Times*, 12 Apr. 2013, https://www.nytimes.com/2013/04/14/fashion/other-popular-youtube-video-producers.html.

POGUE, DAVID. "Internet Memes 101: A Guide to Online Wackiness." *The New York Times*, 8 Sept. 2011, https://pogue.blogs.nytimes.com/2011/09/08/internet-memes-101-a-guide-to-online-wackiness/.

QIN, AMY. "Chinese Censors Have New Target: Celebrity News." *The New*

York Times, 9 June 2017, https://www.nytimes.com/2017/06/09/world/asia/china-celebrity-news-wechat.html.

REN, YUAN. "Know Your Chinese Social Media." *The New York Times*, 19 Nov. 2018, https://www.nytimes.com/2018/11/19/fashion/china-social-media-weibo-wechat.html.

ROOSE, KEVIN. "Don't Scoff at Influencers. They're Taking Over the World." *The New York Times*, 16 July 2019, https://www.nytimes.com/2019/07/16/technology/vidcon-social-media-influencers.html.

ROOSE, KEVIN. "YouTube's Product Chief on Online Radicalization and Algorithmic Rabbit Holes." *The New York Times*, 29 Mar. 2019, https://www.nytimes.com/2019/03/29/technology/youtube-online-extremism.html.

SAFRONOVA, VALERIYA. "James Charles, From 'CoverBoy' to Canceled." *The New York Times*, 14 May 2019, https://www.nytimes.com/2019/05/14/style/james-charles-makeup-artist-youtube.html.

TORREGROSA, LUISITA LOPEZ. "Around the World in 80 Days for Cuba's Most Famous Dissident Blogger." *The New York Times*, 5 Mar. 2013, https://rendezvous.blogs.nytimes.com/2013/03/05/around-the-world-in-80-days-for-cubas-most-famous-dissident-blogger/.

TUCKER, ABIGAIL. "How Cats Evolved to Win the Internet." *The New York Times*, 15 Oct. 2016, https://www.nytimes.com/2016/10/16/opinion/sunday/how-cats-evolved-to-win-the-internet.html.

WAKABAYASHI, DAISUKE. "Inside the Hollywood Home of Social Media's Stars. (Don't Be Shy.)." *The New York Times*, 30 Dec. 2017, https://www.nytimes.com/2017/12/30/business/hollywood-apartment-social-media.html.

WAKABAYASHI, DAISUKE. "YouTube Drops Online Star Logan Paul From Premium Advertising." *The New York Times*, 10 Jan. 2018, https://www.nytimes.com/2018/01/10/technology/logan-paul-youtube.html.

WAKABAYASHI, DAISUKE, ET AL. "Sleeping in Car and Visiting Gun Range: How YouTube Attacker Spent Final Hours." *The New York Times*, 4 Apr. 2018, https://www.nytimes.com/2018/04/04/us/youtube-shooting-nasim-najafi-aghdam.html.

WEISER, BENJAMIN. "Man Who Hacked Celebrities' Email Accounts Gets 5 Years in Prison." *The New York Times*, 6 Dec. 2016, https://www.nytimes.com/2016/12/06/nyregion/alonzo-knowles-celebrity-hacker.html.

WILLIAMS, ALEX. "How Jake Paul Set the Internet Ablaze." *The New York Times*, 8 Sept. 2017, https://www.nytimes.com/2017/09/08/fashion/jake-paul-team-10-youtube.html.

WORTHAM, JENNA. "Drizzy and the New Celebrity Worship." *The New York Times*, 28 May 2015, https://www.nytimes.com/2015/05/31/magazine/drizzy-and-the-new-celebrity-worship.html.

WORTHAM, JENNA. "ROFLThing Draws the Internet Celebrities." *The New York Times*, 25 Jan. 2009, https://bits.blogs.nytimes.com/2009/01/25/roflthing-draws-the-internet-celebrities/.

WORTHAM, JENNA. "The Well-Followed on Social Media Cash In on Their Influence." *The New York Times*, 8 June 2014, https://www.nytimes.com/2014/06/09/technology/stars-of-vine-and-instagram-get-advertising-deals.html.

YUAN, LI. "Learning China's Forbidden History, So They Can Censor It." *The New York Times*, 2 Jan. 2019, https://www.nytimes.com/2019/01/02/business/china-internet-censor.html.

ZINOMAN, JASON. "Bo Burnham, Discovered on the Internet, Now Challenges It." *The New York Times*, 3 June 2016, https://www.nytimes.com/2016/06/04/arts/television/bo-burnham-discovered-on-the-internet-now-challenges-it.html.

Index

This book is current up until the time of printing. For the most up-to-date reporting, visit www.nytimes.com.